Agricultural Accounting

A Practitioner's Guide

Third Edition

Steven M. Bragg

For more information about AccountingTools® products, visit our Web site at www.accountingtools.com.

ISBN-13: 978-1-64221-092-7

Printed in the United States of America

Table of Contents

Preface

Agricultural accounting applies to a large part of the economy, since it includes breeding animals, growing fruits and grains, operating dairies and plant nurseries, raising fish, and so forth. There are a number of unique aspects to agricultural accounting that are not encountered in other industries, including special valuation rules for inventory, hedging transactions, dealing with cooperatives, and recording non-current farm assets. In *Agricultural Accounting*, we address every aspect of the accounting that one might encounter in a farm, ranch, or related business. The intent is to not only explain accounting concepts, but also to provide examples and show how an accounting system can be constructed and operated.

The book is divided into four sections. In Chapters 1 through 4, we cover the essential building blocks of farm accounting, including accrual basis accounting, types of accounts, and the most common accounting transactions. In Chapters 5 through 15, we address the specific accounting for a number of functional areas, including receivables, inventory, fixed assets, and payables. In Chapters 16 and 17, we address the creation of financial statements and the disclosures that accompany them. We also note a number of analyses in Chapter 18 that can be used to improve one's understanding of the financial performance and condition of a farm. Finally, we provide in Chapter 19 an overview of the many tax rules that apply to farmers.

You can find the answers to many questions about agricultural accounting in the following chapters, including:

- Which accounts should a farm accounting system use?
- What are the standard journal entries that a farm accountant is most likely to use?
- How is farm inventory valued?
- What is the proper valuation method for trees and vines?
- What is the best way to account for farm debt?
- What is the accounting for hedging as it applies to farm activities?
- What is the accounting by a farm when dealing with a cooperative?
- What financial statement disclosures does a farm attach to its financial statements?
- Which analyses should be used to extract information from farm financial statements?

Agricultural Accounting is designed for the farm accountant who wants to set up and operate an accounting system that is specific to the needs of a farm, ranch, or similar enterprise.

Centennial, Colorado
August 2022

About the Author

Steven Bragg, CPA, has been the chief financial officer or controller of four companies, as well as a consulting manager at Ernst & Young. He received a master's degree in finance from Bentley College, an MBA from Babson College, and a Bachelor's degree in Economics from the University of Maine. He has been a two-time president of the Colorado Mountain Club, and is an avid alpine skier, mountain biker, and certified master diver. Mr. Bragg resides in Centennial, Colorado. He has written more than 250 books and courses, including *New Controller Guidebook, GAAP Guidebook,* and *Payroll Management.*

Steven maintains the accountingtools.com web site, which contains continuing professional education courses, the Accounting Best Practices podcast, and thousands of articles on accounting subjects.

Chapter 1
Introduction to Agricultural Accounting

Introduction

One of the most crucial aspects of farm management is to understand revenues, expenses, and cash flows. A proper system of accounting is needed to accumulate this information over time, so that each transaction is recorded correctly. Once the accounting information has been recorded, it is summarized into a set of financial statements that can be used to determine the financial results, financial position, and cash flows of a farm. In short, a good accounting system should provide a vehicle for gathering information, from which decisions can be made. The main goal of this book is to show the user how to develop an accounting system that will generate the information needed to properly manage the finances of a farm.

A Note on Terminology

There are many types of operations in the field of agriculture. In order to standardize around a single term, we use the term "farm" as a substitute for all types of agricultural operations, including the following:

- Breeding and feeding cattle, hogs, sheep, and so forth
- Breeding horses
- Growing fruits and nuts
- Growing grains, such as wheat and corn
- Growing vegetable fibers, such as cotton
- Growing vegetables, soybeans, sugarcane, and so forth
- Operating dairies
- Operating plant nurseries
- Operating poultry and egg production plants
- Raising fish and shellfish
- Raising small animals, such as mink and chinchilla

The Economic Entity Concept

An economic entity is a business, so a farm is an economic entity. In accounting, an economic entity is kept separate from the personal transactions of the owner, so that the financial condition of the owner and the business are not intermixed. This means that the accounting records for a farm must exclude any activities related to the owner. For example, if the owner goes on a private trip, the cost of that trip is personal – its cost is not to be included in the financial statements of the farm. Similarly, if the owner buys a truck for personal use and pays for it through the farm entity, that is incorrect

– the farm is suffering a loss of cash while not gaining from the use of the truck. Consequently, under the economic entity concept, the correct treatment of the preceding two examples would be:

- The owner pays for the private trip out of his own pocket. It never appears in the financial records of the farm.
- If the owner needs money to buy the truck, he first records a distribution of money from the farm to his private bank account, and then purchases the truck with these funds. The farm records only indicate a distribution of cash to the owner; no truck appears in its financial records.

The economic entity concept applies to any business, but it is especially applicable to farms. Since many farms are owned by a single individual or family, there is a strong tendency for personal expenses to become intermixed with the operating results of the farm, resulting in a reported farm profitability level that is too low.

Financial Statements

The information produced by an accounting system is summarized into financial statements. These statements are used to gain a summary-level view of different aspects of a farm's financial performance and condition. The financial statements are comprised of three reports, which are:

- *Income statement.* This report shows the revenues generated, expenses incurred that offset the revenues, and the resulting profit or loss for the farm. The information presented in an income statement covers a period of time, such as a month, quarter, or year. This is the most frequently examined financial statement.
- *Balance sheet.* This report shows the assets, liabilities, and equity of a farm as of a specific point in time. The balance sheet is especially important when a farm has a large amount of obligations; it is used to compare the amounts of assets and liabilities, to estimate the ability of the farm to pay off its debts.
- *Statement of cash flows.* This report shows the cash inflows generated by a farm for a period of time, as well as its cash outflows. The ability to generate cash is the ultimate reporting mechanism for a business, so this can be quite a useful document. The cash flow information reported in the statement of cash flows can be significantly different from the profit or loss reported in the income statement, since the two documents report different kinds of information. We will address these differences shortly.

An additional statement that is sometimes created is the statement of owner's equity. This report shows any changes in the owner's interest in the business during the reporting period. It is usually only reported as part of a farm's annual financial statements, so it is not considered to be a core financial statement.

It is important to be aware of the differences in time periods covered by these reports. The income statement, the statement of cash flows, and the statement of owners' equity all report on the activity that occurred over a period of time, while the balance sheet only reports on the financial condition of a farm as of a specific date. For example, if a farm is reporting its results for the month of June, the income statement and the statement of cash flows will contain the results of everything that happened during June, while the balance sheet will only contain information as of the last date of that reporting period, which is June 30.

The financial statements are not just used internally, to manage a farm. They are also required by lenders and creditors. A *lender* is any entity that lends money in exchange for the payment of interest, such as a bank. A *creditor* is a business that allows a farm to pay bills on a later date but without paying interest, such as a farm supply store. Lenders and creditors want to know if a farm operation is a good credit risk, and so will demand a complete set of financial statements before agreeing to extend credit.

Format of the Financial Statements

Each of the financial statements is prepared in a certain format, which differs depending on the industry in which a business operates. For example, the income statement format for a farm differs from the one used by a mining operation, a casino, or a bank. Each of these organizations conducts business in a different way, and so needs to tailor its financial statements to reflect those differences. In the following sub-sections, we show a typical presentation format for each of the financial statements that could be used for a farm.

Income Statement

The income statement presents a summarization of four types of activities in which a farm may engage. They are:

- *Revenues*. This is sales generated from the sale of farm products.
- *Expenses*. This is the costs to produce and sell farm products, as well as other administrative costs of the farm.
- *Gains*. This is any gains generated from the sale of farm assets, such as from the sale of a tractor.
- *Losses*. This is any losses generated from the sale of farm assets, such as from the sale (as before) of a tractor.

When the total amount of revenue and gains exceeds the amount of expenses and losses, a farm earns a profit. When the reverse is the case, the farm has generated a loss. Thus, the calculation of profits and losses in an income statement is:

Revenue + Gains – Expenses – Losses = Net profit or loss

A problem with the income statement is that it includes both *operating activities* and *financing activities*. Operating activities are those items directly associated with the operation of the farm, while financing activities are the costs of loans and the income from investments. These two activities need to be split apart in order to see how well the underlying farming operations are actually performing. For example, a farm could be burdened with a substantial amount of debt, and so must record a large interest expense in its income statement every month, resulting in a reported loss. If the interest expense were to be moved into a different part of the income statement, one might see that the operations were actually making money.

An additional problem is that the income statement can include the results of *investing activities*. For example, the purchase and eventual sale of assets are considered investing activities. When there is a gain or loss on the sale of an asset, the gain or loss appears in the income statement. The reporting of gains and losses can skew the results of a farm, so that its operating results are obscured.

There is no requirement to separate operating, financing, and investing activities in the income statement, but it is a good idea to do so. For example, the income statement could be structured into the general categories appearing in the following exhibit.

Sample Income Statement

+	Farm revenues
-	Operating expenses
=	Operating income
+	Other revenue and gains
-	Other expenses and losses
=	Net income

Explanations of these general categories are as follows:

- *Farm revenues.* This is the money generated from the sale of what a farm produces. For example, the sale of crops, livestock and poultry generate farm revenue, as do the sale of livestock products, such as eggs, milk, and wool.
- *Operating expenses.* This is the cost to operate a farm. Examples of these costs are feed, fertilizer, and the compensation paid to hired employees.
- *Operating income.* This is the difference between farm revenues and operating expenses.
- *Other revenue and gains.* This is all other earnings of the farm, such as interest income and the gain on sale of a farm truck. Thus, this category includes both financing activities and investing activities.
- *Other expenses and losses.* This is all other expenses of the farm, such as interest expense and losses on the sale of farm equipment. Thus, this category also includes both financing activities and investing activities.
- *Net income.* This is operating income, plus other revenue and gains, minus other expenses and losses.

Other general categories may be used instead. The main point is to be consistent in using the same categories over time, so that the results reported in a number of successive income statements can be compared.

Once the general categories of information have been decided upon, additional line items are included within each category to provide more information to the reader. The following exhibit contains a sample income statement format that could be used by a farm operation.

Sample Farm Income Statement

Sales:	
Crops	$250,000
Feeder livestock	300,000
Livestock products	50,000
Agricultural program payments	125,000
Total sales	$725,000
Operating expenses:	
Feeder livestock	$275,000
Purchased feed	140,000
Fertilizer	30,000
Herbicides and pesticides	3,000
Truck and machinery hire	2,000
Wage expense	152,000
Payroll taxes	10,000
Repairs and maintenance	2,000
Utilities expense	17,000
Depreciation expense	13,000
Loss on sale of assets	4,000
Total operating expenses	$648,000
Operating income	77,000
Income taxes	27,000
Net income	$50,000

Statement of Owner's Equity

The statement of owner's equity shows any changes in the owner's interest in the business during the reporting period. The report presentation states the assets that the owner originally and subsequently invested in the farm, minus any assets withdrawn, plus any profits earned, minus any losses incurred. The ending balance in the report is the amount of equity that the farmer has in the business. For example, when a farmer invests $10,000 in his farm, the equity balance increases by $10,000. If the farm generates a profit of $2,000, the equity balance increases by $2,000. If the farm incurs a $4,000 loss, the equity balance decreases by $4,000. The basic format of the statement of owner's equity appears in the following exhibit.

Sample Statement of Owners' Equity

+/-	Beginning equity
+/-	Net income/loss
+	Additional investments in the farm
-	Withdrawals from the farm
=	Ending equity

The beginning equity figure noted in the first row of the report is the ending equity figure from the preceding period (usually as of the end of the last year), so this information is a carry forward from an earlier statement of owner's equity. The net income or loss figure comes from the income statement for the current period. The line item for additional investments in the farm is used to present any more assets that have been added to the farm during the current reporting period by the owner. For example, an owner might contribute a pickup truck to the farm from his personal assets; this would be an additional investment in the farm.

Withdrawals from the farm document any cases in which the owner uses farm cash to pay for personal items, or simply extracts cash or other assets from the business. For example, a farmer uses the farm checking account to buy a $50,000 automobile for his personal use. This is a withdrawal from the farm.

In some years, there may be no additional investments in or withdrawals from the business, so these lines will not appear in the report.

Balance Sheet

The balance sheet is sometimes called the statement of financial position, since it refers to the status (or *position*) of the organization as of a particular point in time. The balance sheet is laid out based on the *accounting equation*, which is as follows:

$$\text{Assets} = \text{Liabilities} + \text{Equity}$$

In essence, the accounting formula states that the grand total of all assets appearing on the balance sheet must exactly match the combined total of all liabilities and equity on the report. The assets classification in the balance sheet can include many items, such as cash, receivables, and fixed assets. The liabilities classification includes the obligations of the farm, such as payables and mortgage debt. The equity section contains the ending equity figure that was just described for the statement of owner's equity.

In the balance sheet, assets and liabilities are listed in order by the amount of time it would usually take to convert them into cash. This is called the *order of liquidity*.

6

Thus, in the assets section, the amount of cash on hand would be reported before the amount of fixed assets. Similarly, in the liabilities section, the amount of accounts payable would be reported before the amount of long-term debt.

There may be a *current assets* heading in the balance sheet. All assets that are expected to be converted into cash within one year are listed within this classification. All assets that will not be converted for a longer period of time are listed under the *non-current assets* heading. Similarly, there may be a *current liabilities* heading in the liabilities section of the balance sheet, as well as a *non-current liabilities* heading. The following exhibit contains a brief example of the format that could be used for a balance sheet, where assets are listed down the left side, while liabilities and equity are listed down the right side. This is a horizontal format. An alternative is the vertical format, in which the assets section is listed first, with liabilities and then equity listed beneath the assets. The vertical approach allows a farm to present information for multiple reporting periods, using as many columns as will fit on the page. The horizontal format is easier to read, but only allows for the presentation of information for one reporting period.

Sample Balance Sheet Layout

ASSETS	LIABILITIES
Current assets	Current liabilities
Cash	Accounts payable
Accounts receivable	Interest payable
Prepaid expenses	Taxes payable
Inventory	Accrued expenses
Total current assets	Current portion of long-term debt
Non-current assets	Total current liabilities
Breeding livestock	Non-current liabilities
Buildings	Mortgages payable
Farm machinery	Deferred taxes
Perennial crops	Total non-current liabilities
Less: Accumulated depreciation	Contributed capital
Total non-current assets	Retained capital
Total assets	Total liabilities and equity

Statement of Cash Flows

The statement of cash flows reveals the inflows and outflows of cash that a farm has experienced during the reporting period. The general format of the statement is to group cash inflows and outflows into three general categories, summarize them, and trace the total amount back to the cash on hand at the end of the period, as stated in the balance sheet.

The statement segregates cash flows into three categories, which are operating activities, investing activities, and financing activities – all of which we have already mentioned. In brief, any cash payments or receipts associated with the daily operations of a farm are classified as *operating activities*. Most cash flows should appear within this category. For example, receiving government payments, receiving cash from the sale of livestock, paying for fertilizer, and paying hired staff all fall into this category. Interestingly, interest payments are also classified as an operating activity.

Investing activities involve the purchase and sale of fixed assets, the purchase and sale of securities for investment purposes, and several similar activities. There are likely to be a few of these transactions each year, so the investing activities section will contain fewer line items than the operating activities section. *Financing activities* involve either the receipt of long-term funds or the repayment of these funds to the other party. The receipt of a loan and its repayment (though not the associated interest) are the transactions most commonly found in the financing activities section.

Once the amounts of operating, investing, and financing cash flows are added together and netted against the beginning cash balance for the reporting period, the result is the ending cash balance. This ending amount matches the cash balance that appears in the balance sheet. The general layout of the statement of cash flows appears in the following exhibit.

Sample Statement of Cash Flows Layout

+/-	Cash flows from operating activities
+/-	Cash flows from investing activities
+/-	Cash flows from financing activities
=	Net increase (decrease) in cash
+	Cash at beginning of period
=	Cash at end of period

This basic format can be greatly expanded to provide additional information about the exact sources and uses of cash. The following exhibit contains a sample statement of cash flows that could be used by a farm operation.

Sample Statement of Cash Flows

Cash flows from operating activities		
Net income		$3,000,000
Adjustments for:		
Depreciation and amortization	$125,000	
Provision for losses on accounts receivable	20,000	
Gain on sale of facility	-65,000	
		80,000
Increase in trade receivables	-250,000	
Decrease in inventories	325,000	
Decrease in trade payables	-50,000	
		25,000
Cash generated from operations		3,105,000
Cash flows from investing activities		
Purchase of fixed assets	-500,000	
Proceeds from sale of breeding livestock	35,000	
Net cash used in investing activities		-465,000
Cash flows from financing activities		
Owner withdrawals	-80,000	
Proceeds from real estate loans	360,000	
Net cash used in financing activities		280,000
Net increase in cash and cash equivalents		2,920,000
Cash and cash equivalents at beginning of period		2,080,000
Cash and cash equivalents at end of period		$5,000,000

Note: Owner withdrawals are considered a financing activity, even though a large part of these withdrawals are probably to compensate the farm family for their labor; wages are normally classified within operating activities.

In the preceding exhibit, we refer to cash equivalents. A *cash equivalent* is a highly liquid investment having a maturity of three months or less. It should be at minimal risk of a change in value. Examples of cash equivalents are marketable securities, money market funds, and short-term government bonds.

Financial Statement Disclosures

A complete set of financial statements also includes a number of disclosures, which may be referred to as footnotes. These disclosures clarify and expand upon certain line items noted in the financial statements, and supply other information. Disclosures are usually added to the annual financial statements that are issued to outsiders, and not to the more abbreviated monthly financial statements. Disclosures are covered in the Financial Statement Disclosures chapter.

Construction of Financial Statements

Accounting software packages are widely available and quite inexpensive. Consequently, there is no need to manually track accounting transactions and then laboriously construct financial statements. Instead, the accounting software comes with a pre-configured set of financial statement report layouts, so that the farm accountant merely has to select a report option in order to print the statements.

The only real issue involving the construction of financial statements is to exercise a proper degree of caution when revising the standard financial statement report template. There is a risk that adding or subtracting report line items will result in some accounts being listed more than once or not at all.

Tip: When creating customized financial statements in an accounting package's report writer module, test them by printing the standard "boilerplate" version and comparing these results to the information appearing in the customized version. If the totals are different, then the customized statements are probably wrong.

Additional Commentary on the Financial Statements

The format used for each of the preceding financial statements should not change from period to period. By adopting a highly consistent approach to recording information, one can trace changes in each of the line items of the financial statements over time, picking out spikes and dips in the numbers that can be indicators of problems or opportunities that should be investigated.

The income statement and the statement of cash flows report on the results of a business for a full year. This is called the *fiscal year*, and can span any 12-month period. This period does not have to correspond to the calendar. For example, a farmer could choose to have a fiscal year that begins on February 1 and ends on January 31 of the following year. Using the example, the income statement and statement of cash flows will start aggregating results as of February 1, and will stop doing so on January 31 of the next year. At that point, these two reports are reset to have zero balances, and will start accumulating information for the next fiscal year.

The balance sheet and the statement of owner's equity are not zeroed out at the end of each fiscal year. Instead, these two reports continue to roll forward their balances into each successive reporting period. For example, a farm's balance sheet reports the amount of accounts payable that it currently owes to suppliers; in each successive balance sheet, the payables balance will be reduced for all payments made to suppliers and increased by all new invoices received from suppliers.

Profits vs. Cash Flows

After having perused the preceding discussion about the financial statements, one might note that the income statement reports on profitability, while the statement of cash flows reports on cash flows. What is the difference?

Profitability occurs when total revenues exceed total expenses. Positive cash flows occur when total cash inflows exceed total cash outflows. These two amounts can vary substantially, to the point where a farm may report profits and yet experience negative cash flows (and vice versa). Here are several issues that can cause disparities between the two figures:

- An expense may be recognized in the income statement, even though the supplier or employee has not yet been paid. This happens under the accrual basis of accounting, which we will discuss in the next chapter.
- Revenue may be recognized in the income statement, even though the customer has not yet paid. Again, this happens under the accrual basis of accounting.
- A farm may pay a substantial amount for a new asset, such as a tractor, which causes a large cash outflow. However, the related expense is spread out in the income statement over a number of years.
- A farm pays a large amount of cash to pay down a loan. This does not appear in the income statement.
- The family that owns a farm draws a large amount from the farm's cash account for its own living expenses. This does not appear in the income statement.

Which of the two measures is more important? Definitely cash flow. The primary focus is always on having sufficient cash to pay the bills, so the farm accountant should always know exactly how much cash is available, when more cash is coming in, and when cash is expected to be paid out. That being said, a farm must consistently report profits over the long term. When this is the case, lenders are more willing to provide loans, and buyers are more willing to offer a reasonable price to buy a farm.

This discussion of profits versus cash flows can leave a farmer wondering how to discern the level of success of his farm, especially if profit levels and cash flows are presenting two different views. A simple way to make this determination is to look at a combination of three items, which are:

- The trend in indebtedness of the farm
- The trend in the age of farm assets
- The reasonableness of owner withdrawals

If the farm is consistently paying down its outstanding debt while still replacing and improving upon the farm's assets and paying a reasonable amount to the farm family

11

in the form of owner withdrawals, then it is reasonable to assume that the farm is doing well.

Accounting Principles

Lenders, creditors, and owners want the financial statements of a farm to fairly present its financial condition. For this to happen, the accounting profession has come up with a number of accounting principles that serve as a guideline for how to record information and prepare financial statements. We already introduced the economic entity concept, where the accounting for a business is kept separate from the accounting for its owners. Here are several more accounting principles:

- *Conservatism principle.* This principle states that expenses and liabilities should be recorded as soon as possible, but that revenues and assets are to be recorded only when there is a high degree of certainty that they will occur. This principle introduces a conservative slant to the financial statements that may yield lower reported profits, since the recognition of revenue and assets may be delayed for some time. Conversely, this principle tends to encourage the recognition of losses earlier, rather than later. The concept can be taken too far, where a business persistently misstates its results to be worse than is really the case.
- *Consistency principle.* This principle states that, once an accounting method is adopted, it should continue to be used until a demonstrably better method comes along. Not following this principle means that an organization could continually jump between different accounting treatments of its transactions that make its long-term financial results quite difficult to discern.
- *Cost principle.* This principle states that a business should only record its assets and liabilities at their original purchase prices. This principle is becoming less valid, as a host of accounting standards are heading in the direction of adjusting assets and liabilities to their fair values. The principle was originally followed because purchase prices are easily proven.
- *Full disclosure principle.* This principle states that one should include in an entity's financial statements all of the information that would affect a reader's understanding of those statements. To comply with this principle, it may be necessary to add disclosure footnotes to the financial statements.
- *Going concern principle.* This principle states that the financial statements are constructed on the assumption that an organization will remain in operation for the foreseeable future. This means that a farm would be justified in deferring the recognition of some expenses (such as depreciation) to a later period. If an organization were not to remain in business for long, then these expenses would instead be recognized at once, possibly resulting in the recognition of losses.
- *Matching principle.* This principle states that, when a business records revenue, it should also record all related expenses at the same time. By doing so,

someone reading the financial statements does not have to worry that the profits reported in the current period are inflated.

- *Materiality principle.* This principle states that a transaction should be recorded in the accounting records if not doing so might alter the decision-making process of someone reading the firm's financial statements. This principle is difficult to follow in practice; overly conservative accountants tend to use it as an excuse to record even the smallest items in the accounting records.
- *Reliability principle.* This principle states that only those transactions that can be proven should be recorded. For example, a supplier invoice is solid evidence that an expense has been recorded. This concept is of great interest to auditors, who need to see evidence to prove that a farm's financial statements are accurate. This information comes from source documents, which are the original documents that contain the details of business transactions. Examples of source documents are checks, deposit slips, and invoices.
- *Revenue recognition principle.* This principle states that a business should only recognize revenue when it has substantially completed the earnings process. Otherwise, revenue is reported too soon, which overstates the amount of profits that were actually earned.

When creating financial statements, most transactions will be standard, ongoing items for which there is a history of recording the accounting information in the same way, every time. The real issue arises when an unusual transaction comes up that has not been seen before, or very rarely. In these latter situations, apply the preceding principles to see if doing so provides clarity to the best way to account for them (if at all).

A further consideration is the amount of usefulness to be gained by recording additional accounting information. If the cost of recording and reporting information exceeds the usefulness of the information, then it may make sense to not record the information. When there is any doubt, consult with the farm's certified public accountant for advice.

The Certified Public Accountant

We just noted that, when there is a question about how to deal with an accounting issue, one can ask the farm's certified public accountant, or CPA. This person is an independent accountant who has passed the CPA exam and also fulfilled an experience requirement, which is set by the local state government. A CPA's primary role is to examine the accounting records of a business and issue a certifying statement that the firm's financial statements are a fair representation of its financial results and condition.

A lender is likely to require that a CPA examine the accounting records and financial statements of a farm, if the farm has a loan outstanding with the lender or is requesting one. In addition to this service, one can also contact the CPA for advice, as well as for assistance with tax filings.

Accounting Standard-Setting Organizations

Where do the accounting rules come from? They are called accounting standards, and they are created by two organizations. One is the Financial Accounting Standards Board (FASB), which has created a massive set of accounting standards for entities operating within the United States. Actually, the FASB is the latest in a series of organizations that have been creating and refining accounting standards for many decades. A farm operating within the United States will likely need to create financial statements that comply with the accounting standards issued by the FASB. The entire set of these standards, taken as a whole, is referred to as Generally Accepted Accounting Principles, or GAAP.

The other organization that creates accounting standards is the International Accounting Standards Board (IASB). The IASB has constructed the International Financial Reporting Standards, or IFRS. Most of the world other than the United States complies with IFRS. If a farm is located outside of the United States or is owned by a foreign entity, it is likely that the farm's financial statements will be constructed using IFRS.

There are only a few major differences between GAAP and IFRS, though there are numerous smaller differences. The organizations have been working to reduce these differences for a number of years. It does not appear that the FASB and IASB will ever completely settle their differences, so it seems likely that there will be two different sets of accounting standards for the foreseeable future.

In addition to GAAP and IFRS, the Farm Financial Standards Council (FFSC) produces *Financial Guidelines for Agriculture*. The FFSC recognizes that many farm operations are small and do not have the resources to maintain their accounting records in accordance with GAAP. The *Guidelines* are intended to standardize the use of financial reports, financial criteria and measures, and information management by farming operations, providing a reporting alternative and supplement to GAAP. Though the *Guidelines* are not recognized by GAAP, we will make note of them at times in this text and identify them as being part of the *Guidelines*, rather than GAAP.

Lenders, creditors, and investors want farms to closely follow either GAAP or IFRS, so that they can more easily compare the financial statements of many organizations. When everyone follows the same rules when conducting their accounting, their financial statements should be quite comparable. For example, this means that a lender could compare the results of an agricultural operation to those of a peer group to see how it is performing against a baseline. This comparison then tells the lender whether it should loan funds to the firm.

Financial Accounting and Managerial Accounting

There are two types of accounting. One is called financial accounting, and focuses on the process used to record business transactions and convert this information into financial statements. Financial accounting is the primary focus of this book. The other type of accounting is managerial accounting, which involves collecting, analyzing, and reporting information about the operations and finances of a business. These reports are directed to the managers of the business, rather than to any outside parties such as lenders or creditors.

There are a number of differences between financial and managerial accounting, which fall into the following categories:

- *Aggregation.* Financial accounting reports on the results of an entire business. Managerial accounting frequently reports at a more detailed level, such as the profits earned from a particular crop.
- *Efficiency.* Financial accounting reports on the profitability (and therefore the efficiency) of a business, whereas managerial accounting reports on specifically what is causing problems and how to fix these issues.
- *Reporting focus.* Financial accounting is oriented toward the creation of financial statements. Managerial accounting is more concerned with operational reports, which are only distributed internally.
- *Standards.* Financial accounting must comply with the various accounting standards, whereas managerial accounting does not have to comply with any standards when it compiles information for internal consumption.
- *Time period.* Financial accounting is concerned with the financial results that a business has already achieved, so it has a historical orientation. Managerial accounting may address budgets and forecasts, and so can have a future orientation.
- *Timing.* Financial accounting requires that financial statements be issued following the end of an accounting period. Managerial accounting may issue reports much more frequently, since the information it provides is of most relevance if managers can see it right away.

There is certainly a place for both financial and managerial accounting in an agriculture-oriented business. Many managers prefer to see managerial accounting reports, since these reports are more likely to contain specific, actionable items.

Summary

In this chapter, we have provided the farmer with a high-level overview of accounting principles, the entities that create accounting standards, the different types of accounting, and the nature of the financial statements. By carefully perusing a farm's financial statements, one can gain an understanding of the farm's performance, its ability to survive, and the types of cash receipts and payments that it is making. We will return to the examination of financial statements in a later chapter; in the next two chapters, we will clarify the building blocks of the financial statements, which means discussing cash and accrual basis accounting, as well as accounts and how they are recorded in the accounting system.

Chapter 2
Accrual and Cash Basis Accounting

Introduction

The accounting specified in this book is based on the concept of accrual basis accounting. Some knowledge of accounting is needed to use the accrual basis. Many farmers are understandably more interested in operating a farm than in learning about the details of accounting, and so may be using the simpler cash basis of accounting. In this chapter, we describe each of these types of accounting, and how to convert accounting books constructed under the cash basis to the accrual method.

Cash Basis of Accounting

In a smaller farm that does not have a trained farm accountant, it is quite common to use the cash basis of accounting. The cash basis is the practice of only recording revenue when cash is received from a customer, and recording expenses only when cash has been paid out. This approach has the key advantage of being intuitively simple to use, since it does not vary much from the practice of keeping a checkbook. In addition, the results of a cash-basis system can be transferred with few modifications directly into a tax return. Further, a farm manager can elect to accelerate some payments under the cash basis, thereby increasing the amount of recorded expenses and reducing the amount of reported taxable profits in the current period. However, the cash basis of accounting also suffers from the following problems:

- *Accuracy.* The cash basis yields less accurate results than the accrual basis of accounting (which is explained next), since the timing of cash flows does not necessarily reflect the proper timing of changes in the financial condition of a business. For example, if a contract with a customer does not allow a farm to issue an invoice for a significant period of time, the farm will be unable to report any revenue until the invoice has been issued and cash received.
- *Manipulation.* A farm accountant can alter a farm's reported results by not cashing received checks or by altering the payment timing for liabilities.
- *Lending.* Lenders do not feel that the cash basis generates overly accurate financial statements, and so may refuse to lend money to a farm reporting under the cash basis.
- *Audited financial statements.* Auditors will not certify financial statements that were compiled under the cash basis, so a farm will need to convert to the accrual basis if it wants to have audited financial statements.
- *Management reporting.* Since the results of cash basis financial statements can be inaccurate, management reports should not be issued that are based upon it.

A possible option is for a smaller farm to begin keeping its books under the cash basis, and then switch to the accrual basis of accounting when it has grown to a sufficient size to warrant the extra accounting expertise.

Accrual Basis of Accounting

The accrual basis of accounting is the concept of recording revenues when earned and expenses as incurred. For example, a farm operating under the accrual basis of accounting will record a sale as soon as it sells livestock at an auction, while a cash basis farm would instead wait to be paid before it records the sale. Similarly, an accrual basis farm will record an expense as incurred, while a cash basis farm would instead wait to pay its supplier before recording the expense. In effect, the difference between the cash and accrual methods is the timing of when revenues and expenses are reported.

EXAMPLE

The year-end of a farm is December 31. On December 29, the farm manager receives an offer from the manager of a neighboring farm to buy several feeder calves for $800. The calves are delivered on December 30, and the check paying for the calves arrives in the mail on January 3rd. Under the accrual basis of accounting, the sale is recorded in the prior year, even though the cash was not received until the next year. Under the cash basis of accounting, the sale is not recorded until the cash is received.

The accrual basis of accounting is advocated under both Generally Accepted Accounting Principles and International Financial Reporting Standards. Both of these sets of accounting standards provide guidance regarding how to account for revenue and expense transactions in the absence of the cash receipts or payments that would trigger the recordation of a transaction under the cash basis of accounting.

The accrual basis tends to provide more even recognition of revenues and expenses over time than the cash basis, and so is considered to be the most valid accounting system for ascertaining the results of operations, financial position, and cash flows of a farm. In particular, it supports the matching principle, under which revenues and all related expenses are to be recorded within the same reporting period; by doing so, it should be possible to see the full extent of the profits and losses associated with certain sales within a single reporting period.

The accrual basis requires the use of estimated reserves in certain areas. For example, a farm should recognize an expense for estimated bad debts that have not yet been incurred. By doing so, all expenses related to a revenue transaction are recorded at the same time as the revenue, which results in an income statement that fully reflects the results of operations. These estimates may not be entirely accurate, and so can lead to materially inaccurate financial statements. Consequently, a considerable amount of care must be used when estimating reserves.

The manager of a smaller farm may elect to avoid using the accrual basis of accounting, since it requires a certain amount of accounting expertise. Also, the owner may choose to manipulate the timing of cash inflows and outflows to create a smaller amount of taxable income under the cash basis of accounting, which can result in the deferral of income tax payments.

A significant failing of the accrual basis is that it can indicate the presence of profits, even though the associated cash inflows have not yet occurred. The result can be a supposedly profitable farm that is starved for cash, and which may therefore go bankrupt despite its reported level of profitability.

Accrual-Adjusted Approach

The Farm Financial Standards Council advocates the use of the accrual-adjusted approach, which is a hybrid of the cash basis and accrual basis. Under the accrual-adjusted approach, the farmer maintains his accounting records using the cash basis of accounting, and then makes certain adjustments to the records at the end of the year. The key adjustments are:

- Accrual adjustments are made to the books to bring them into alignment with the results expected under the accrual basis.
- The value of inventory is recorded at year-end, which does not occur under the cash-basis method.

By using the accrual-adjusted approach, a farm manager will have cash-basis financial statements for 11 months of the year; these statements will not be as accurate as accrual-basis statements, and so will provide less useful information.

Because the accrual-adjusted approach does not result in sufficiently accurate financial statements for 11 out of 12 monthly financial statements per year, we do not recommend its use. For the remainder of this book, we will instead show how the accrual basis of accounting is used.

Converting Cash Basis to Accrual Basis Accounting

A farm manager may want to convert his accounting records from the cash basis to the accrual basis of accounting. This is needed when the financial statements are to be audited, or when an investor or lender wants to see accrual-basis financial statements. To convert from cash basis to accrual basis accounting, follow these steps:

- *Add accrued expenses*. Add back all expenses for which the farm has received a benefit but has not yet paid the supplier or employee. This means one should accrue for all types of expenses, such as wages earned but unpaid, feed received but unpaid, and so forth.
- *Subtract cash payments*. Subtract cash expenditures made for expenses that should have been recorded in the preceding accounting period. This also means reducing the beginning equity balance, thereby incorporating these expenses into the earlier reporting period.
- *Add prepaid expenses*. Some cash payments may relate to assets that have not yet been consumed, such as rent deposits. Review expenditures made during

the accounting period to see if there are any prepaid expenses, and move the unused portion of these items into an asset account. If the same approach is taken for expenditures made in prior periods, adjust the beginning equity balance to remove the expenses that are now being shifted into a prepaid expenses asset account.

- *Add accounts receivable*. Record accounts receivable and sales for all billings issued to customers and for which no cash has yet been received from them.
- *Subtract cash receipts*. Some sales originating in a prior period may have been recorded within the current accounting period based on the receipt of cash in that period. If so, reverse the sale transaction and record it instead as a sale and account receivable in the preceding period. This will require an adjustment to the beginning equity account.

The conversion of cash basis to accrual basis accounting can be a difficult one, for any accounting software that has been configured for the cash basis is not designed to handle accrual basis accounting. This means that all conversion adjustments must be made manually, with journal entries. It may be easier to manage the conversion on a separate spreadsheet, and never include it in the formal accounting records at all.

It is quite possible that some transactions will be missed during the conversion from cash basis to accrual basis accounting. Unfortunately, the only way to be certain of a complete and accurate conversion is to examine all accounting transactions during the year being converted, as well as in the final quarter of the preceding year. Thus, the conversion is both labor-intensive and expensive.

Further, a very complete set of accounting records is required to convert from the cash basis to the accrual basis. Since a farm already on the cash basis is likely to be a small one with less funding for accounting support, it is quite possible that the accounting records are in a sufficient state of disarray that the conversion cannot be made in a reliable manner.

Summary

Simply stated, the cash basis of accounting is the easiest way to account for farm transactions. It is intuitively simple, and so can be handled by someone with no formal accounting expertise. Nonetheless, cash basis financial statements cannot be audited, and many lenders require audited financial statements. Given this key issue, the following chapters are entirely concerned with how to account for a farm under the accrual basis of accounting.

Chapter 3
Accounts

Introduction

There are several levels of information in an accounting system. Financial statements, as described in a preceding chapter, sit at the top-most level. All of the information in the accounting system rolls up into the financial statements. At the bottom of this pyramid are the accounts in which information is stored. In this chapter, we discuss accounts, their nature, and how they are used.

Transactions

The accounting system begins with transactions. A transaction is a business event that has a monetary impact on a farm's financial statements, and which is recorded as an entry in its accounting records. Examples of transactions are:

- Paying a supplier for services rendered or goods delivered
- Paying an employee for hours worked
- Receiving a payment from the government

We will refer to transactions many times in this chapter, since the ongoing recordation of transactions is essential for maintaining the accounting records.

Accounts

An account is a record in a system of accounting that contains all of the activities related to one of the following:

- A type of revenue
- A type of expense
- A type of asset
- A type of liability
- A type of equity
- A type of gain
- A type of loss

The explanations of these items are as follows:

- *Revenue*. This is an increase in the assets or a decrease in the liabilities of a business, which is caused by the provision of goods or services to customers. It is a quantification of the gross activity generated by a business.
- *Expense*. This is the reduction in value of an asset as it is consumed to generate revenue. Many costs are charged to expense as soon as they are incurred. In other cases, they will not be consumed for a period of time, and so will be charged to expense over multiple reporting periods.
- *Asset*. This is an item of economic value that is expected to yield a benefit in future periods.
- *Liability*. This is a legally binding obligation that is payable to another entity.
- *Equity*. This is the net amount of assets invested in a business by its owners, plus any retained earnings.
- *Gains and losses*. This is the difference between the book value of an asset and the price obtained when it is sold. Book value is the amount at which an asset is recorded in the accounting records of a farm.

The accounting system for a farm may include a relatively small number of accounts if its operations are simple. However, as a farm operation expands in size and scope, there may be so many different activities going on that the farmer will need to know more about the farm's financial performance and condition; if so, he may subdivide accounts in order to store information at a more refined level. For example, a farm may begin with a single account for cash, which is intended to reflect the presence of a single checking account. Over time, the farmer decides to open two more bank accounts for various reasons. When this happens, a separate account is needed in the accounting system for each bank account. These separate accounts are needed in order to more easily track the contents of each bank account.

The general rule for creating each additional account is to only do so if the resulting information is useful. If not, the extra effort expended to maintain the account is just a waste of time. For example, a farmer starting up quite a small farm begins with a single expense account, which he calls Farm Operating Expenses. He receives little insight from this account, since virtually all of the farm's expenses are being recorded in the same place. After a few months, he decides to add several expense accounts. One is for compensation expense, another is for maintenance expenses, and a third is for herbicides expense. All other farm expenses are still recorded within the Farm Operating Expenses account. Transactions related to compensation, maintenance, and herbicides are stored in the new accounts. With this additional level of refinement, the farmer has more knowledge of certain aspects of the farm's operations, which he can (presumably) use to increase its efficiency.

There are no requirements in the accounting standards for using certain accounts, though there are a number of accounts that are frequently found in the accounting systems of farms, based on common usage.

When researching accounting information, the best place to start is the account, since it stores transaction details. A sample account appears in the following exhibit, where the detail is listed for the accounts payable account. The record contains five columns, which list the following information:

- *Date*. This is the date on which the transaction was recorded. The earliest transaction appears at the top, and the latest at the bottom.
- *Description*. This is a few words describing the nature of the transaction.
- *Debits*. Debits are explained in the Double Entry Accounting section later in this chapter. In the exhibit, the account is a liability account, where payments made to *reduce* the liability are stated as debits.
- *Credits*. As just noted, credits are explained in a later section. In the exhibit, the account is a liability account, so the receipt of additional liabilities results in the entry of credits to *increase* the account balance.
- *Balance*. This column contains a running total of the balance in the account. In the exhibit, the beginning balance appears in the first row. Each entry thereafter adds to or subtracts from the beginning balance.

Sample Detailed Accounts Payable Account

Accounts Payable				
Date	Description	Debits	Credits	Balance
Jan. 1	Beginning balance			-$24,500.00
Jan. 3	Plains Farm Supply invoice		2,800.00	27,300.00
Jan. 5	Lakeside Pesticides invoice		463.00	27,763.00
Jan. 7	Payments issued	$3,142.00		24,621.00
Jan. 7	Kenny's Lumber Supply invoice		348.00	24,969.00

An account record may contain an additional column that identifies the source document. A *source document* is the physical basis upon which a transaction is based. For example, an adjustment to the cash account is likely based on the statement sent from the farm's bank. Therefore, the bank statement is a source document. Or, in the preceding example, a supplier invoice is the source document. Source documents usually contain the following information:

- A description of the transaction
- The date of the transaction
- A specific amount of money
- An authorizing signature (in some cases)

Accounts are stored in a ledger. A *ledger* is the entire set of accounts used for a farming operation. Most accounting is now conducted in a computerized accounting system, where a general ledger contains all accounts. In a small farm operation, accounts may instead be maintained manually. If so, each account is listed on a separate ledger page; one can then flip through the ledger to find every transaction in which the farm was engaged.

The Chart of Accounts

Accounts are listed in the *chart of accounts*, which is a simple columnar listing of every account used by a farm. A chart of accounts is created as part of the process of constructing an accounting system. The chart typically begins with a relatively small number of accounts, which should be sufficient for a smaller farm operation. As the farm increases in size and complexity over time, accounts can be added to the chart of accounts in order to keep track of additional items.

Accounts are listed in the chart of accounts in order by how they will appear in the financial statements. The general order is:

1. Assets
2. Liabilities
3. Equity
4. Revenue
5. Expenses
6. Gains and losses

Thus, asset accounts are listed first, followed by liability accounts, and so on. The following exhibit contains a sample chart of accounts. The chart only contains an account number for each account and the name of the account. The sample contains accounts that would be used by a farm that engages in growing crops and raising livestock, so it may contain more accounts than a more specialized farm might need.

Sample Chart of Accounts

Account Number	Account Description
1000	Cash
1010	Investments
1100	Accounts Receivable
1200	Prepaid Expenses
1300	Inventory – Barley
1310	Inventory – Breeding Livestock
1320	Inventory – Feed
1330	Inventory – Feeder Livestock
1340	Inventory – Wheat
1400	Cash Investment in Growing Crop
1410	Breeding Livestock
1500	Buildings
1510	Land
1520	Office Furniture and Equipment

Accounts

Account Number	Account Description
1530	Perennial Crops
1540	Tractors
1550	Vehicles
1600	Accumulated Depreciation
1700	Investments in Cooperatives
1710	Other Investments
2000	Accounts Payable
2010	Payroll Taxes Payable
2020	Taxes Payable
2030	Interest Payable
2040	Notes Payable – Short-term
2050	Notes Payable – Long-term
3000	Contributed Capital
3010	Retained Capital
3020	Owner Withdrawals
4000	Sales – Agricultural program payments
4010	Sales – Crops
4020	Sales – Feeder Livestock
4030	Sales – Livestock Products
4040	Crop Insurance Proceeds
4050	Change in Value of Crop Inventory
4060	Change in Value of Raised Breeding Livestock
5000	Feeder Livestock
5010	Purchased Feed
5020	Fertilizer
5030	Herbicides and Pesticides
5040	Gas, Fuel and Oil
5050	Veterinarian and Medical Expense
5060	Wage Expense
5070	Payroll Tax Expense
5080	Equipment Repairs
5090	Utilities Expense
5100	Insurance Expense
5110	Hedging Expense

Account Number	Account Description
5120	Depreciation Expense
5130	Interest Expense
5140	Interest Income
5150	Income Tax Expense
5160	Real Estate Taxes
5170	Personal Property Taxes
6000	Miscellaneous Income
7000	Gain/Loss on Sale of Fixed Assets

In the preceding exhibit, we have included some separation between the account numbers. For example, the account number for the Buildings account is 1500, while the number for the next account is 1510. The reason for this separation is to keep a sufficient amount of room to insert more accounts. For example, if there were to be a need for a Computer Software account, it could be assigned number 1505, which slots it between the Buildings account and the Land account.

In the preceding exhibit, we have set each class of accounts to begin with a separate number. For example, asset account numbers begin with a "1," while liability account numbers begin with a "2," and so forth. This is a standard numbering convention that is common in many industries. The farm accountant does not need to follow this numbering scheme, but it is an easy way to identify the nature of an account.

The expenses portion of the chart of accounts is subject to a considerable amount of expansion. The farm accountant can add accounts to reflect other activities, such as truck and machinery hire, breeding fees, shearing, wool twine and sacks, and so forth.

Account Descriptions

To assist in deciding whether to use an account, we have provided a number of account descriptions in this section, along with commentary on how applicable they may be, depending on the circumstances. The account descriptions are as follows:

Current Assets (for assets expected to last less than one year)

- *Cash.* Used to record all cash transactions, where the ending account balance should equal the amount of cash on hand. A separate account should be used for cash on hand, each checking account, each savings account, and so forth.
- *Investments.* Used to record all types of investments, such as in marketable securities. If an investment is in a cooperative, it may be classified as a non-current asset, which would call for the use of a separate investments account within that classification.
- *Accounts receivable.* Used to record all sales of grain, livestock, and other products for which the associated cash payment has not yet been received.

- *Prepaid expenses*. Used to record all expenditures made for items that have not yet been consumed, such as prepaid insurance. These amounts are charged to expense as consumed.
- *Inventory – breeding livestock*. Used to record the value of livestock that has been raised for sale. This livestock is not intended for use in the herd. There may be a different account for each type of livestock.
- *Inventory – [crop name]*. Used to record the value of raised or purchased crops that will be sold within the next year. A separate account can be used for each type of crop.
- *Inventory – feed*. Contains the value of the feed currently on hand that will be used within the next year to feed livestock. Separate accounts could be used to designate grown feed and purchased feed.
- *Inventory – feeder livestock*. Contains the value of all types of livestock that are being fattened in a feedlot, with the intention of selling them. There can be multiple accounts here; for example, there could be a separate account for each type of animal, and/or to designate whether animals were purchased or raised.
- *Cash investment in growing crop*. This account contains the ongoing cost of growing perennial crops. Once sales are recognized, these costs are taken from the account and charged to expense.

Non-Current Assets (for assets expected to last one year or more)

- *Breeding livestock*. Contains the value of any breeding livestock to be used in the herd. This account does not contain the value of any livestock designated for sale as market animals.
- *Buildings*. Includes the cost to acquire or construct all farm buildings, including sheds and silos. This account may be redesignated as Buildings and Improvements, so that the costs of fencing, ditches, ponds, and related items can be stored in it.
- *Land*. Includes the cost to acquire land, as well as the costs to make permanent upgrades to the land, such as clearing, leveling, and terracing. These costs are not depreciated, so be careful about deciding what to include in this account.
- *Office equipment and furniture*. Used to record the purchase cost of many kinds of furniture and office equipment, such as computers, storage cabinets, and desks.
- *Perennial crops*. Includes the costs to acquire perennial plants and maintain them.
- *Tractors*. Contains the purchase costs of all farm tractors. This account can be combined with the following Vehicles account if there is a relatively small amount of farm machinery. A Machinery account could be used instead.
- *Vehicles*. Contains the purchase costs of all farm vehicles. This account can be combined with the preceding Tractors account if there is a relatively small amount of farm machinery. A Machinery account could be used instead.

- *Accumulated depreciation.* This account shows the cumulative amount of depreciation expense that has been charged against existing assets. A separate accumulated depreciation account can be set up for each class of asset, but only do so if the resulting information is useful.
- *Investments in cooperatives.* This account contains the amount of cash and other assets invested in farm cooperatives.
- *Other investments.* This account is used to record the cost of land that has been acquired for speculative purposes, as well as other investments that are not expected to be liquidated within the next year.

All of the preceding accounts are classified as asset accounts. However, the accumulated depreciation account is somewhat different. It is called a *contra account*, because it is paired with and offsets the fixed asset accounts. The balance in a normal asset account (as noted in the Double Entry Accounting section) is a debit, but the normal balance in the accumulated depreciation account is a credit. The balances in the other fixed asset accounts are all stated at their original costs, so the accumulated depreciation balance is offset against them to arrive at a net book value for the fixed assets.

Current Liabilities (for liabilities that are payable in less than one year)

- *Accounts payable.* Contains the amount of all unpaid invoices received from suppliers. For example, the account may contain an invoice for diesel fuel delivered to a farm.
- *Payroll taxes payable.* Contains the balance of all payroll taxes not yet submitted to the government. This account contains both the farm's payroll tax obligations and the amount of any payroll taxes owed by employees, which the farm subtracted from their pay and will remit to the government on their behalf.
- *Taxes payable.* Includes the amounts of several types of taxes owed, such as personal property taxes, property taxes, income taxes, and local levies.
- *Interest payable.* Contains the amount of interest payable to lenders and lessors for outstanding loans and leases, respectively.
- *Notes payable – short-term.* Contains just that portion of long-term debt that is payable within one year, as well as any loans that must be paid off in the next year. The purpose behind this account is to properly classify debt on the farm's balance sheet.

Non-current Liabilities (for liabilities that are payable in one year or more)

- *Notes payable – long-term.* Contains all debt owed by the farm, other than the amount classified as being short-term. If there are several loans, it can make sense to track each one in a separate account, to ensure that each one is paid in a timely manner.

Equity

- *Contributed capital.* Contains the amounts invested in the farm operation by its owners.
- *Retained capital.* This is a catchall account that includes all other equity transactions, including the cumulative amount of net income generated by the farm.
- *Owner withdrawals.* This account tracks reductions in the owner's equity that are caused by the withdrawal of cash or other assets from the farm business. Withdrawals are typically made to pay for the living expenses and personal taxes of the family running a farm. This account is not used when a farm is organized as a corporation; in that case, distributions are instead made using dividends.

> **Note:** The Farm Financial Standards Council recommends that the owner withdrawals account be split into two accounts. One is called "Owner Withdrawals for Unpaid Labor and Management," (for use as the name implies) while the other account is called "Other Distributions," and is intended to show excess additional distributions.

Revenue

- *Agricultural program payments.* Contains all payments received from government assistance programs for which there is no obligation to make a return payment.
- *Sales - Crops.* Contains the revenue generated from the sale of crops during the reporting period. This account could be broken down into a separate account for each type of crop sold.
- *Sales - Feeder livestock.* Contains the revenue generated from the sale of feeder livestock (which have been fattened in a feedlot).
- *Sales - Livestock products.* Contains the revenue generated from the sale of livestock products, such as eggs, milk, and wool. A separate account could be used for each product.
- *Crop insurance proceeds.* Contains the amounts paid to the farm by insurers in compensation for crop damage.
- *Change in value of crop inventory.* This account states the change in value (up or down) caused by the change in total value of a farm's crop inventory that is being held for sale at the end of the reporting period.
- *Change in value of raised breeding livestock.* This account states the change in value (up or down) caused by the change in total value of raised breeding livestock that is being held for sale at the end of the reporting period.

Expenses

- *Feeder livestock.* This account records the cost of feeder calves, pigs, poultry, and lambs. These costs are charged to expense because the livestock has been sold.

- *Purchased feed.* This account contains the cost of all purchased feed that was consumed during the reporting period.
- *Fertilizer.* Contains the amount of fertilizer consumed by the farm in the reporting period.
- *Herbicides and pesticides.* Contains the amount of herbicides and pesticides consumed by the farm in the reporting period.
- *Gas, fuel, and oil.* Contains the cost of the gas, fuel, and oil delivered to and consumed by the farm.
- *Veterinarian and medical expense.* Contains the cost of veterinarian fees and medications incurred by the farm in the reporting period.
- *Wage expense.* Contains the cost of salaried and hourly staff.
- *Payroll tax expense.* Contains that portion of payroll taxes paid by the farm.
- *Equipment repairs.* Contains the cost incurred to repair and maintain farm equipment.
- *Utilities expense.* Contains the cost of all utilities, including water, electricity, sewage, and Internet access.
- *Insurance expense.* Can contain several types of insurance, such as crop damage insurance, property insurance, and medical insurance for the staff.
- *Hedging expense.* Contains the cost of any hedging instruments purchased that are being used to offset potential commodity price declines.
- *Depreciation expense.* Contains the amount of depreciation charged against fixed assets to date for the current year.
- *Interest expense.* Contains the year-to-date amount of interest expense that the farm incurred on its debt.
- *Interest income.* Contains the income received on the farm's invested funds.
- *Income tax expense.* Contains the amount of income tax expense obligation that the farm has incurred thus far in its fiscal year.
- *Real estate taxes.* Contains the amount of taxes charged to the farm on the value of its land and buildings.
- *Personal property taxes.* Contains the amount of taxes charged to the farm for its movable property, such as trucks and tractors.
- *Miscellaneous income.* Acts as a catchall account for all other sources of income that are not related to the operations of the farm.
- *Gain/loss on sale of fixed assets.* Contains the difference between the net book value of fixed assets and the price at which the assets were then sold to a third party.

It can be useful to periodically examine the chart of accounts and see if it should be expanded or reduced. When accounts only contain a small balance or are rarely examined, it could make sense to merge them into a related account. Conversely, if the farm manager is routinely wading through large numbers of transactions within an account in order to find information, it could make sense to sub-divide the account into two or more accounts that are more precisely targeted at certain kinds of transactions.

Double Entry Accounting

Double entry accounting is a record keeping system under which every transaction is recorded in at least two accounts. There is no upper limit on the number of accounts used in a transaction, but the minimum is two accounts. There are two columns in each account, with debit entries on the left and credit entries on the right. In double entry accounting, the total of all debit entries must match the total of all credit entries. When this happens, a transaction is said to be *in balance*. If the totals do not agree, the transaction is *out of balance*. An out of balance transaction must be corrected before financial statements can be created.

The definitions of a debit and credit are:

- A debit is an accounting entry that either increases an asset or expense account, or decreases a liability or equity account. It is positioned to the left in an accounting entry.
- A credit is an accounting entry that either increases a liability or equity account, or decreases an asset or expense account. It is positioned to the right in an accounting entry.

Characteristics of Sample Accounts

Account Name	Account Type	Normal Account Balance
Cash	Asset	Debit
Accounts receivable	Asset	Debit
Inventory	Asset	Debit
Fixed assets	Asset	Debit
Accounts payable	Liability	Credit
Notes payable	Liability	Credit
Contributed capital	Equity	Credit
Retained capital	Equity	Credit
Revenue	Revenue	Credit
Cost of goods sold	Expense	Debit
Compensation expense	Expense	Debit
Utilities expense	Expense	Debit
Gain on sale of asset	Gain	Credit
Loss on sale of asset	Loss	Debit

The key point with double entry accounting is that a single transaction always triggers a recordation in *at least* two accounts, as assets and liabilities gradually flow through a business and are converted into revenues, expenses, gains, and losses. We expand upon this concept in the next section.

The Accounting Equation

The *accounting equation* is the basis upon which the double entry accounting system is constructed. In essence, the accounting equation is:

$$Assets = Liabilities + Owner's\ Equity$$

The assets in the accounting equation are the resources that a farm has available for its use, such as cash, accounts receivable, fixed assets, and inventory. The farm pays for these resources by either incurring liabilities (which is the Liabilities part of the accounting equation) or by obtaining funding from the owners (which is the Owner's Equity part of the equation). Thus, there are resources with offsetting claims against those resources, either from creditors or owners.

The Liabilities part of the equation is usually comprised of accounts payable that are owed to suppliers, a variety of other liabilities, such as income taxes, and debt payable to lenders.

The Owner's Equity part of the equation is more complex than simply being the amount paid to the farm by its owners. It is actually their initial investment, plus any subsequent gains, minus any subsequent losses, minus any owner withdrawals.

This relationship between assets, liabilities, and owner's equity appears in the balance sheet, where the total of all assets always equals the sum of the liabilities and shareholders' equity sections.

The reason why the accounting equation is so important is that it is *always* true - and it forms the basis for all accounting transactions. At a general level, this means that whenever there is a recordable transaction, the choices for recording it all involve keeping the accounting equation in balance.

EXAMPLE

Creekside Orchard engages in the following series of transactions:

1. Creekside sells shares to an investor for $10,000. This increases the cash (asset) account as well as the capital (equity) account.
2. Creekside buys $4,000 of cider from a supplier. This increases the inventory (asset) account as well as the payables (liability) account.
3. Creekside sells the cider for $6,000. This decreases the inventory (asset) account and creates a cost of goods sold expense that appears as a decrease in the income (equity) account.
4. The sale of Creekside's inventory also creates a sale and offsetting receivable. This increases the receivables (asset) account by $6,000 and increases the income (equity) account by $6,000.
5. Creekside collects cash from the customer to which it sold the cider. This increases the cash (asset) account by $6,000 and decreases the receivables (asset) account by $6,000.

Accounts

These transactions appear in the following table.

Item	(Asset) Cash	(Asset) Receivables	(Asset) Inventory		(Liability) Payables	(Equity) Capital	(Equity) Income
(1)	$10,000			=		$10,000	
(2)			$4,000	=	$4,000		
(3)			-4,000	=			-$4,000
(4)		$6,000		=			6,000
(5)	6,000	-6,000		=			
Totals	$16,000	$0	$0	=	$4,000	$10,000	$2,000

In the example, note how every transaction is balanced within the accounting equation - either because there are changes on both sides of the equation, or because a transaction cancels itself out on one side of the equation (as was the case when the receivable was converted to cash).

The following table shows how a number of typical accounting transactions are recorded within the framework of the accounting equation.

Sample Accounting Transaction Entries

Transaction Type	Assets	Liabilities + Equity
Buy fixed assets on credit	Fixed assets increase	Accounts payable (liability) increases
Buy inventory on credit	Inventory increases	Accounts payable (liability) increases
Pay rent	Cash decreases	Income (equity) decreases
Pay supplier invoices	Cash decreases	Accounts payable (liability) decreases
Sell goods on credit (part 1)	Inventory decreases	Income (equity) decreases
Sell goods on credit (part 2)	Accounts receivable increases	Income (equity) increases
Sell stock	Cash increases	Equity increases

Here are examples of each of the preceding transactions, where we show how they comply with the accounting equation:

- *Buy fixed assets on credit.* Creekside buys a machine on credit for $10,000. This increases the fixed assets (asset) account and increases the accounts payable (liability) account. Thus, the asset and liability sides of the transaction are equal.
- *Buy inventory on credit.* Creekside buys cider on credit for $5,000. This increases the inventory (asset) account and increases the accounts payable (liability) account. Thus, the asset and liability sides of the transaction are equal.

32

- *Pay rent.* Creekside pays $4,000 in rent. This reduces the cash (asset) account and reduces the accounts payable (liabilities) account. Thus, the asset and liability sides of the transaction are equal.
- *Pay supplier invoices.* Creekside pays $29,000 on existing supplier invoices. This reduces the cash (asset) account by $29,000 and reduces the accounts payable (liability) account. Thus, the asset and liability sides of the transaction are equal.
- *Sell goods on credit.* Creekside sell cider for $55,000 on credit. This increases the accounts receivable (asset) account by $55,000 and increases the revenue (equity) account. Thus, the asset and equity sides of the transaction are equal.
- *Sell stock.* Creekside sells $120,000 of its shares to investors. This increases the cash account (asset) by $120,000 and increases the capital stock (equity) account. Thus, the asset and equity sides of the transaction are equal.

Journal Entries

A journal entry is a formalized method for recording a business transaction. It is recorded in the accounting records of a business, usually in the general ledger, but sometimes in a subsidiary ledger that is then summarized and rolled forward into the general ledger.

Journal entries are used in a double entry accounting system, where the intent is to record every business transaction in at least two places. For example, when a farm sells crops for cash, this increases both the revenue account and the cash account. Or, if a pig is purchased on account, this increases both the accounts payable account and the feeder livestock account.

The structure of a journal entry is:

- A header line may include a journal entry number and entry date.
- The first column includes the account number and account name into which the entry is recorded. This field is indented if it is for the account being credited.
- The second column contains the debit amount to be entered.
- The third column contains the credit amount to be entered.
- A footer line may also include a brief description of the reason for the entry.

Thus, the basic journal entry format is:

	Debit	Credit
Account name / number	$xx,xxx	
Account name / number		$xx,xxx

The structural rules of a journal entry are that there must be a minimum of two line items in the entry, and that the total amount entered in the debit column equals the total amount entered in the credit column.

A journal entry is usually printed and stored in a binder of accounting transactions, with backup materials attached that justify the entry. This information may be accessed by the farm's auditors as part of their annual audit activities.

There are several types of journal entries, including:

- *Adjusting entry*. An adjusting entry is used at month-end to alter the financial statements to bring them into compliance with the relevant accounting standards. For example, a farm could accrue unpaid wages at month-end in order to recognize the wages expense in the current period.
- *Compound entry*. This is a journal entry that includes more than two lines of entries. It is frequently used to record complex transactions, or several transactions at once. For example, the journal entry to record a payroll usually contains many lines, since it involves the recordation of numerous tax liabilities and payroll deductions.
- *Reversing entry*. This is an adjusting entry that is reversed as of the beginning of the following period, usually because an expense was accrued in the preceding period, and is no longer needed. Thus, a wage accrual in the preceding period is reversed in the next period, to be replaced by an actual payroll expenditure.

In general, journal entries are not used to record high-volume transactions, such as customer billings or supplier invoices. These transactions are handled through specialized software modules within the accounting software that present a standard online form to be filled out. Once the form is complete, the software automatically creates the accounting record.

The Trial Balance

The trial balance is a report run at the end of a reporting period. It is primarily used to ensure that the total of all debits equals the total of all credits, which means that there are no unbalanced journal entries in the accounting system that would make it impossible to generate accurate financial statements. Printing the trial balance to match debit and credit totals has fallen into disuse, since accounting software rejects the entry of unbalanced journal entries.

The trial balance can also be used to manually compile financial statements, though with the predominant use of computerized accounting systems that create the statements automatically, the report is rarely used for this purpose.

When the trial balance is first printed, it is called the *unadjusted trial balance*. Then, when the farm accountant corrects any errors found and makes adjustments to bring the financial statements into compliance with the accounting standards, the report is called the *adjusted trial balance*.

A trial balance report contains the following columns of information:

1. Account number
2. Account name
3. Ending debit balance (if any)
4. Ending credit balance (if any)

Each line item only contains the ending balance in an account, which comes from the general ledger. All accounts having an ending balance are listed in the trial balance; usually, the accounting software automatically blocks all accounts having a zero balance from appearing in the report, which reduces its length. A sample (and highly simplified) trial balance follows:

Sample Trial Balance

Account Number	Account Description	Debit	Credit
1000	Cash	$60,000	
1100	Accounts receivable	180,000	
1330	Inventory – feeder livestock	300,000	
1500	Buildings	210,000	
2000	Accounts payable		$90,000
2030	Interest payable		50,000
2050	Notes payable – Long-term		420,000
3010	Retained capital		350,000
4020	Sales – feeder livestock		400,000
5000	Feeder livestock	290,000	
5060	Wage expense	200,000	
5070	Payroll tax expense	20,000	
5090	Utilities expense	35,000	
5160	Real estate taxes	15,000	
	Totals	$1,310,000	$1,310,000

Summary

Each farm will create its own unique chart of accounts that is built around the characteristics of its operations and the level of detail that the farm manager wants to see. We recommend that the initial chart of accounts suggested by the accounting software provider could be worth retaining with a few adjustments, as long as the pre-set accounts are targeted at agricultural operations. Otherwise, a local CPA firm could be consulted for advice on what accounts are typically used for the farm's specific operations.

Chapter 4
Accounting Transactions

Introduction

The farm accountant will likely find that certain transactions will be repeated many times over the course of a year. In this chapter, we discuss the journal entries needed to record these transactions. While the information in this chapter will not address *all* farm-related transactions, they will cover a significant proportion of the total number, and should at least provide clues for how to proceed with more rarely-encountered transactions.

The journal entries in this chapter are clustered into three transaction types. The first is financing activities, which can involve the initial formation of a farm with an owner investment, as well as such other transactions as owner withdrawals and obtaining a loan. We then describe investing activities, such as the purchase or sale of assets, asset exchanges, and asset leases. Finally, we note a number of journal entries related to operating activities. These include entries for the purchase of livestock and crops, feed purchases, and supplies – essentially activities directly associated with the core farm operations. We then address more general operational entries, such as the recordation of payroll and taxes. We finish with a discussion of the entries related to farm revenue.

Financing Activities

The owners of farms will probably need to invest funds and other assets in a farm when it is first started, and possibly at intervals thereafter. They may also withdraw funds from the business for various reasons. In addition, a farm manager may borrow money from a lender in order to pay for various operations or assets, as well as pay back these loans over time. All of these actions are financing activities. In this section, we describe a number of journal entries related to financing activities.

Owner Investments

The owners of a business may invest cash or other assets in the farm. The essential accounting is to debit the asset accounts to which the owners are making additions, and to credit the equity account to show the amount being invested in the business. For example, a $10,000 cash investment in a farm would result in the following entry:

	Debit	Credit
Cash [asset account]	10,000	
Contributed capital [equity account]		10,000

Or, an owner might acquire a used truck and employ it for farm activities. The entry to record such a truck in the accounting records of the farm is:

	Debit	Credit
Vehicles [asset account]	15,000	
Contributed capital [equity account]		15,000

A more complex owner investment transaction appears in the following example, where multiple assets are used to start a farm.

EXAMPLE

Tom Mayberry plans to start a farm. He invests $150,000 of his personal savings in the new operation. He also contributes a used truck that is worth $20,000, plus $5,000 of computer equipment and 50 breeding cows that have a market value of $30,000. These investments result in the following journal entry:

	Debit	Credit
Cash [asset account]	150,000	
Breeding livestock [asset account]	30,000	
Office furniture and equipment [asset account]	5,000	
Vehicles [asset account]	20,000	
Contributed capital [equity account]		205,000

In the example, the used assets are initially recorded on the books of the farm at their market values. The grand total of the assets that have been added is the amount of capital being invested in the business. Note that, in the resulting journal entry, the total of all debits equals the total credits.

Associated Liabilities

The owners may contribute an asset to the farm business that has a liability associated with it. For example, a tractor with a value of $50,000 is contributed to a farm; the owner had originally purchased the tractor with a $20,000 loan. The amount of the liability is recorded on the books of the farm along with the tractor asset. The two amounts are netted together to arrive at the $30,000 of contributed capital that is recorded as part of the transaction. The resulting journal entry is:

	Debit	Credit
Tractors [asset account]	50,000	
Notes payable [liability account]		20,000
Contributed capital [equity account]		30,000

As another example, the owners have purchased a $3,000 computer on credit, and now contribute the computer to the farm. The associated liability to pay for the computer has not yet been paid. The resulting journal entry is for the computer asset and an offsetting account payable. Since the two entries net to zero, there is no additional entry into the contributed capital account. The journal entry is:

	Debit	Credit
Office furniture and equipment [asset account]	3,000	
Accounts payable [liability account]		3,000

Owner Withdrawals

In a smaller farming operation, it is relatively common for the owner of a farm to commingle accounts, which means that personal expenses are paid from the farm's bank account. Doing so is not recommended, since it is more difficult to determine the true profitability of the business. If these transactions are expected to continue, the correct accounting treatment is *not* to record the personal expenditures as expenses of the farm. Instead, they are recorded as owner withdrawals.

For example, an owner does not have enough cash in his personal checking account to make the $2,000 monthly mortgage payment on his house, and so elects to pay the bank from his farm's checking account. The entry removes cash from the business and reduces the owner's equity in the business by a similar amount. The journal entry is:

	Debit	Credit
Owner withdrawals [equity account]	2,000	
Cash [asset account]		2,000

Loans

Farmers routinely borrow money from lenders to finance a farm's operations and/or fixed asset purchases. This involves signing a promissory note in which the loan amount is stated, as well as the interest rate that will be charged. When the loan is initiated, the lender sends cash to the farm, which results in an increase in the farm's cash balance and an offsetting loan liability. In the following sample journal entry, we assume that the loan amount is $250,000. The entry is:

	Debit	Credit
Cash [asset account]	250,000	
Notes payable – long-term [liability account]		250,000

In the last entry, we assumed that the loan would be long-term, where loan repayment would continue for several years. If the loan had instead been a short-term one (as would be the case for a loan intended to cover short-term needs until the next harvest) the liability would instead be credited to a short-term notes payable account. For example:

	Debit	Credit
Cash [asset account]	250,000	
Notes payable – short-term [liability account]		250,000

The farm manager will make a series of monthly payments to pay down the amount owed under a promissory note. Each of these payments is comprised of two components, which are principal and interest. The amount of interest paid is the interest rate multiplied by the remaining principal balance, so the proportion of each loan payment that is comprised of interest is quite high for earlier payments and much lower in later payments, after the remaining principal balance has declined. For example, a farm manager receives a loan statement from the bank, noting that a loan payment is due in the amount of $1,200. Of this amount, $750 is interest and $450 is principal repayment. The associated journal entry is:

	Debit	Credit
Interest expense [expense account]	750	
Notes payable – long-term [liability account]	450	
Cash [asset account]		1,200

Investing Activities

Any farm requires a certain amount of ongoing investment, either to replace worn-out equipment or to expand its operations. In this section, we describe a number of investing activities and the related journal entries.

Asset Acquisitions

A farm manager may acquire a number of assets to support farm operations. For example, a silo is constructed by a contractor, a tractor is purchased from a dealer, a truck is bought at auction, and breeding livestock is bought from another farm operation. In all cases, an asset account is credited for the purchase price of the asset. There are two choices for where to credit the offsetting amount. If the purchase was made in cash, then the cash account is credited. If the seller is financing the sale, then a notes payable account is credited. For example, a farm manager buys a tractor for $80,000, using cash. The journal entry is:

	Debit	Credit
Tractors [asset account]	80,000	
Cash [asset account]		80,000

If the dealer had been willing to finance the purchase, the farm manager could instead have bought the tractor under the terms of a promissory note, which would have resulted in this entry:

	Debit	Credit
Tractors [asset account]	80,000	
Notes payable – long-term [liability account]		80,000

Or, what if the dealer had required a 25% down payment? Then the entry would have involved both a reduction in cash and the incurrence of a note payable. The entry would be:

	Debit	Credit
Tractors [asset account]	80,000	
Cash [asset account]		20,000
Notes payable – long-term [liability account]		60,000

Asset Sales

When an asset is sold, the farm receives cash or a note in exchange. If the amount of this payment from the buyer is greater than the book value of the asset, then the farm experiences a gain. If the payment is less than the asset's net book value, then the farm incurs a loss. Net book value is the amount at which an asset is recorded in a farm's accounting records, minus the amount of depreciation already charged against the asset. The concept is expanded upon in the following example.

EXAMPLE

Hillside Farms owns a tractor that originally cost $85,000. Since its purchase, Hillside has recorded $62,000 of depreciation expense on the tractor. This means the net book value of the tractor has now been reduced to $23,000 (calculated as $85,000 purchase price - $62,000 depreciation). The farm manager finds a buyer for the tractor, who is willing to pay $29,000 in cash. The resulting journal entry is:

	Debit	Credit
Cash [asset account]	29,000	
Accumulated depreciation [contra asset account]	62,000	
Tractors [asset account]		85,000
Gain on sale of fixed assets [gain/loss account]		6,000

In the preceding example, the tractor asset account is credited in order to remove the tractor asset from the farm's accounting records. Similarly, the accumulated

40

depreciation account (which normally has a credit balance) is debited in order to re-move the tractor's accumulated depreciation from the records. The cash account in-creases to reflect the receipt of cash from the buyer. When these three items are netted, the result is a gain on sale of the tractor; gains are stated as credits, so the $6,000 gain appears in the journal entry.

In the next example, we restate the sale price in order to generate a loss on the sale of the tractor.

EXAMPLE

We restate the preceding example. The tractor was in unusually poor condition, so the buyer was only willing to pay $14,000 for it. The result would be a loss of $9,000, as noted in the following journal entry:

	Debit	Credit
Cash [asset account]	14,000	
Accumulated depreciation [contra asset account]	62,000	
Loss on sale of fixed assets [gain/loss account]	9,000	
Tractors [asset account]		85,000

Asset Exchanges

A farm manager might trade in an asset as part of the purchase of a replacement asset. The trade-in allowance offered by the seller is essentially the sale price of the old asset, so there is likely to be a gain or loss on the transaction, calculated in roughly the same manner just described for an asset sale. The concept is described in the fol-lowing example.

EXAMPLE

A farm manager wants to trade in a Ford truck at the local dealer for a similar model. The new truck will cost $38,000. The dealer offers an $8,000 trade-in allowance on the old truck, which leaves $30,000 to be paid by the farm manager in cash. The book value of the old truck is $11,000, which is calculated as the original purchase price of $33,000 minus $22,000 of de-preciation. The journal entry to record this transaction is:

	Debit	Credit
Vehicles [asset account]	38,000	
Accumulated depreciation [contra asset account]	22,000	
Loss on sale of fixed assets [gain/loss account]	3,000	
Vehicles [asset account]		33,000
Cash [asset account]		30,000

In the preceding example, there are really two transactions. One is the purchase of a new truck and the other is the sale of the old truck. The transactions are combined, since one will not happen without the other.

Asset Leases

A common arrangement is for a farm to lease some of its assets. A lease is an arrangement where the lessor agrees to allow the lessee to use an asset for a stated period of time in exchange for one or more payments. The lessee can designate a lease as either a finance lease or an operating lease. In essence, a *finance lease* designation implies that the lessee has purchased the underlying asset (even though this may not actually be the case), while an *operating lease* designation implies that the lessee has obtained the use of the underlying asset for only a period of time.

A central concept of the accounting for leases is that the lessee should recognize the assets and liabilities that underlie each leasing arrangement, no matter what type of lease it may be. This concept results in the following recognition in the balance sheet of the lessee as of the lease commencement date:

- Recognize a liability to make lease payments to the lessor
- Recognize a right-of-use asset that represents the right of the lessee to use the leased asset during the lease term

As of the commencement date of a lease, the lessee measures the liability and the right-of-use asset associated with the lease. These measurements are derived as follows:

- *Lease liability.* The present value of the lease payments, discounted at the discount rate for the lease. This rate is the rate implicit in the lease when that rate is readily determinable. If not, the lessee instead uses its incremental borrowing rate.
- *Right-of-use asset.* The initial amount of the lease liability, plus any lease payments made to the lessor before the lease commencement date, plus any initial direct costs incurred, minus any lease incentives received.

EXAMPLE

Riverview Farm enters into a five-year lease, where the lease payments are $35,000 per year, payable at the end of each year. Riverview incurs initial direct costs of $8,000. The rate implicit in the lease is 8%.

At the commencement of the lease, the lease liability is $139,745, which is calculated as $35,000 multiplied by the 3.9927 rate for the five-period present value of an ordinary annuity. The right-of-use asset is calculated as the lease liability plus the amount of the initial direct costs, for a total of $147,745.

When a lessee has designated a lease as an operating lease, the lessee should recognize the following over the term of the lease:

- A lease cost in each period, where the total cost of the lease is allocated over the lease term on a straight-line basis
- Any variable lease payments that are not included in the lease liability
- Any impairment of the right-of-use asset

EXAMPLE

Nimble Farm enters into an operating lease in which the lease payment is $25,000 per year for the first five years and $30,000 per year for the next five years. These payments sum to $275,000 over ten years. Nimble will therefore recognize a lease expense of $27,500 per year for all of the years in the lease term.

When a lessee has designated a lease as a finance lease, it should recognize the following over the term of the lease:

- The ongoing amortization of the right-of-use asset
- The ongoing amortization of the interest on the lease liability
- Any variable lease payments that are not included in the lease liability
- Any impairment of the right-of-use asset

The amortization period for the right-of-use asset is from the lease commencement date to the earlier of the end of the lease term or the end of the useful life of the asset.

After the commencement date, the lessee increases the carrying amount of the lease liability to include the interest expense on the lease liability, while reducing the carrying amount by the amount of all lease payments made during the period. The interest on the lease liability is the amount that generates a constant periodic discount rate on the remaining liability balance.

After the commencement date, the lessee reduces the right-of-use asset by the amount of accumulated amortization and accumulated impairment (if any).

EXAMPLE

Oklahoma Steer Breeding (OSB) agrees to a five-year lease of equipment that requires an annual $20,000 payment, due at the end of each year. At the end of the lease period, OSB has the option to buy the equipment for $1,000. Since the expected residual value of the equipment at that time is expected to be $25,000, the large discount makes it reasonably certain that the purchase option will be exercised. At the commencement date of the lease, the fair value of the equipment is $120,000, with an economic life of eight years. The discount rate for the lease is 6%.

OSB classifies the lease as a finance lease, since it is reasonably certain to exercise the purchase option and buy the equipment.

The lease liability at the commencement date is $84,995, which is calculated as the present value of five payments of $20,000, plus the present value of the $1,000 purchase option payment, discounted at 6%. OSB recognizes the right-of-use asset as the same amount, since there are no initial direct costs, lease incentives, or other types of payments made by OSB, either at or before the commencement date.

OSB amortizes the right-of-use asset over the eight-year expected useful life of the equipment, under the assumption that it will exercise the purchase option and therefore keep the equipment for the eight-year period.

As an example of the subsequent accounting for the lease, OSB recognizes a first-year interest expense of $5,100 (calculated as 6% × $84,995 lease liability), and recognizes the amortization of the right-of-use asset in the amount of $10,624 (calculated as $84,995 ÷ 8 years). This results in a lease liability at the end of Year 1 that has been reduced to $70,095 (calculated as $84,995 + $5,100 interest - $20,000 lease payment) and a right-of-use asset that has been reduced to $74,371 (calculated as $84,995 - $10,624 amortization).

By the end of Year 5, which is when the lease terminates, the lease liability has been reduced to $1,000, which is the amount of the purchase option. OSB exercises the option, which settles the remaining liability. At that time, the carrying amount of the right-of-use asset has declined to $31,875 (reflecting five years of amortization at $10,624 per year). OSB shifts this amount into a fixed asset account, and depreciates it over the remaining three years of its useful life.

The accounting described here for leases is much more complex than had previously been the case, when the lease designations were for operating leases and capital leases. Consider contacting a certified public accountant to set up the exact journal entries needed to recognize leases under the new accounting standards.

Investments in Perennial Crops

Perennial plants, such as are found in an orchard, are usually purchased and then cared for during a multi-year period before they begin commercial production. During this development period, the costs incurred to purchase and maintain the plants are recorded in the Perennial Crops asset account.

A number of costs may be incurred to acquire and maintain perennial plants, including the following:

- Purchase price of the plants
- Farm supplies
- Hired labor
- Payroll taxes

EXAMPLE

Wilkinson Orchards acquires apple rootstock for a new apple orchard that it is developing. The development period is five years. During that time, Wilkinson incurs costs for fertilization, spraying, weeding, and pruning. Most of these development costs are labor-related, though Wilkinson buys fertilizer from a local farm supply store. The following costs relate to the orchard in the first year:

- $15,000 for apple rootstock
- $1,000 for fertilizer
- $20,000 for hired farm labor
- $1,800 for payroll taxes

These incurred costs are translated into the following journal entry:

	Debit	Credit
Perennial crops [asset account]	37,800	
Fertilizer expense [expense account]		1,000
Wage expense [expense]		20,000
Payroll tax expense [expense]		1,800
Cash [asset account]		15,000

In the preceding example, the assignment of certain costs to the perennial crops asset account has gone through a two-step allocation. The fertilizer expense, wage expense, and payroll tax expense were likely charged on the first pass, on the assumption that these costs were related to current operations, and so should be charged to expense as incurred. Once the farm accountant realized that these expenses were to be allocated to the perennial crops asset account, he shifted them out of the expense accounts (which is why they are credited) and into the asset account. However, the $15,000 purchase of apple rootstock would have been immediately obvious as a charge to the perennial crops account, so the $15,000 cash reduction to pay for the rootstock was included in the journal entry. The cash payment associated with the other expenditures is not noted in the journal entry, since the payment would have taken place earlier, before there was any recognition that the expenditures were associated with the perennial crops asset account.

Operating Activities

Operating activities occur far more frequently than the financing and investing entries discussed thus far. These activities can include the incurrence of payment liabilities in order to buy farm supplies and related items, which later translate into the sale of crops and livestock. In this section, we describe a number of journal entries related to purchases, as well as the different transactions involved with product sales to third parties.

Purchases of Market Livestock and Crops

A farm manager may elect to buy market livestock, poultry, or grain and then sell them at a later date. When these purchases are made (perhaps at auction or from a dealer), the price at which the transaction is recorded is the amount paid to the seller. The purchase is made into inventory, from which the items will later be sold.

EXAMPLE

A farm manager attends a local auction and pays $10,000 for feeder pigs, as well as $2,500 for wheat. The resulting journal entry is:

	Debit	Credit
Inventory – feeder livestock [asset account]	10,000	
Inventory – wheat [asset account]	2,500	
Cash [asset account]		12,500

When these inventory items are later sold, they are charged to expense. We will deal with this transaction later, when we get to the sale of livestock and crops.

Annual Costs for Producing Perennial Crops

Once perennial crops have reached the point of commercial production, all costs related to the crops (such as for cultivation, pruning, and spraying) are charged directly to expense as incurred.

EXAMPLE

The apple orchard that a farm manager planted five years ago has now reached commercial production. In the current year, the farm manager pays $750 for fertilizer and $500 for pesticides. Both of these expenditures are charged to expense as incurred. The bill will be paid at a later date. The resulting journal entry is:

	Debit	Credit
Fertilizer [expense account]	750	
Herbicides and pesticides [expense account]	500	
Accounts payable [liability account]		1,250

Feed Purchases

A farm manager may buy feed, such as hay or pellets. This amount can be recorded as inventory, but involves tracking the amount of feed still on hand at the end of each reporting period to determine how much feed has been used, and therefore should be charged to expense. An easier solution is to charge the cost of feed directly to expense. The latter approach is especially relevant when the amount of feed kept on hand is relatively low.

EXAMPLE

A farm manager spends $1,500 for feed at the local farm supply store and buys it on account; that is, the farm will pay the bill at a later date. The resulting journal entry is:

	Debit	Credit
Purchased feed [expense account]	1,500	
Accounts payable [liability account]		1,500

Supplies Purchases

If a farm has established credit with the local farm supply store or pays with a credit card, it is incurring an account payable whenever it makes a purchase, rather than paying cash up front.

EXAMPLE

A farm manager spends $400 on spare parts at the local farm supply store, as well as $550 on fertilizer and $25 for lubricating oil. The resulting journal entry is:

	Debit	Credit
Equipment repairs [expense account]	400	
Gas, fuel, and oil [expense account]	25	
Fertilizer [expense account]	550	
Accounts payable [liability account]		975

If the items in the preceding entry had instead been paid with cash, the final row in the journal entry would have been changed from accounts payable to cash.

Once items on account are paid with cash, the accounts payable account is reduced with a debit entry, while the cash account is reduced with a credit entry. Thus, if the payables amount in the preceding example were to be paid at a later date, the entry would be:

	Debit	Credit
Accounts payable [liability account]	975	
Cash [asset account]		975

Billed Expenditures

A farm will be billed for any number of services and administrative items, such as veterinarian charges, crop insurance fees, and utilities. All of these invoices are dealt with in the same way – by recording them as expenses that are offset by the accounts payable liability account.

EXAMPLE

A farm manager receives three bills in the mail. One is from the farm's veterinarian, for $250 of services. Another is for the farm's monthly $300 crop insurance, while the third invoice is a $525 electricity bill from the local utility. He records these invoices in the accounting system with the following entry:

	Debit	Credit
Veterinarian and medical expense [expense account]	250	
Insurance expense [expense account]	300	
Utilities expense [expense account]	525	
Accounts payable [liability account]		1,075

Prepaid Expenses

A farm may sometimes buy something in advance and use it over a period of time. For example, a farm manager may want to acquire crop insurance, which is payable in advance of the coverage period. This expenditure is initially recorded as an asset, since the coverage period has not yet begun. During the coverage period, the asset is gradually charged to expense.

EXAMPLE

A farm manager elects to pay $12,000 in advance for crop insurance, which will cover the farm's crops for the next 12-month period. The initial entry to record this payment is stated in the following entry:

	Debit	Credit
Prepaid expenses [asset account]	12,000	
Cash [asset account]		12,000

In the first month of the coverage period, $1/12^{th}$ of the total insurance amount is consumed, which results in the following entry:

	Debit	Credit
Insurance expense [expense account]	1,000	
Prepaid expenses [asset account]		1,000

The same entry is used in each of the next 11 months to charge the remaining amount of the prepaid expenses asset to expense.

The same entries just noted for crop insurance can be used for any type of prepayment, such as medical insurance and rent payments.

Payroll

A farm manager may hire a number of laborers who are paid on an hourly basis. In a larger operation, several salaried workers may also be on staff to deal with a variety of administrative tasks. When the periodic payroll is calculated, both hourly and salaried employees must be paid, along with a variety of payroll taxes.

This entry usually includes debits for wages and the farm's portion of payroll taxes. There will also be credits to a number of other accounts, each one detailing the liability for payroll taxes that have not been paid, as well as for the amount of cash already paid to employees for their net pay. The basic entry is:

	Debit	Credit
Wages expense [expense account]	xxx	
Payroll tax expense [expense account]	xxx	
Cash [asset account]		xxx
Federal withholding taxes payable [liability account]		xxx
Social security taxes payable [liability account]		xxx
Medicare taxes payable [liability account]		xxx
Federal unemployment taxes payable [liability account]		xxx
State withholding taxes payable [liability account]		xxx
State unemployment taxes payable [liability account]		xxx
Garnishments payable [liability account]		xxx

The reason for the payroll taxes expense line item in this journal entry is that the farm incurs the cost of matching the social security and Medicare amounts paid by employees, and directly incurs the cost of unemployment insurance. The employee-paid portions of the social security and Medicare taxes are not recorded as expenses; instead, they are liabilities for which the farm has an obligation to remit cash to the taxing government entity.

A key point with this journal entry is that the wages expense contains employee gross pay, while the amount actually paid to employees through the cash account is their net pay. The difference between the two figures (which can be substantial) is the amount of deductions from their pay, such as payroll taxes and withholdings to pay for benefits.

There may be a number of additional employee deductions to include in this journal entry. For example, there may be deductions for 401(k) pension plans, health insurance, life insurance, vision insurance, and for the repayment of employee advances.

When withheld taxes and the farm's portion of payroll taxes are paid at a later date, use the following entry to reduce the balance in the cash account and eliminate the balances in the liability accounts:

	Debit	Credit
Federal withholding taxes payable [liability account]	xxx	
Social security taxes payable [liability account]	xxx	
Medicare taxes payable [liability account]	xxx	
Federal unemployment taxes payable [liability account]	xxx	
State withholding taxes payable [liability account]	xxx	
State unemployment taxes payable [liability account]	xxx	
Garnishments payable [liability account]	xxx	
Cash [asset account]		xxx

Thus, when a farm initially deducts taxes and other items from an employee's pay, the farm incurs a liability to pay the taxes to a third party. This liability only disappears from the farm's accounting records when it pays the related funds to the entity to which they are owed.

Taxes

In addition to the preceding expenditures, a farm must also pay income and property taxes. Income taxes may need to be submitted to the government on a quarterly basis, based on the estimated amount of total income that will be earned for the year. This is usually recorded at the same time as the payment, so the format of the entry is:

	Debit	Credit
Income tax expense [expense account]	xxx	
Cash [asset account]		xxx

The exact structure of real estate taxes will vary by county. A common approach is for the county to send out a billing once a year, for payment several months later, perhaps with an option to pay in several installments. In this case, cash is not paid at once, so the accounts payable account is credited instead. The format of this entry is:

	Debit	Credit
Real estate taxes [expense account]	xxx	
Accounts payable [liability account]		xxx

Sale of Farm Products

A farm sells livestock and crops on an ongoing basis, perhaps at auction or to a cooperative that handles the marketing and eventual sale of products to third parties. The price that the farm receives will depend on the market price as of the sale date, which may be further adjusted for the quality of the product. When payment is received, the farm accountant debits the cash account to record the receipt of cash, while crediting the applicable revenue account that best classifies the nature of the sale. If the farm does not receive payment at the time of sale, the debit is not to the cash account, but rather to the accounts receivable account.

EXAMPLE

A farm manager sells his farm's wheat for $10,000. Payment in cash is made at the point of sale. The resulting journal entry is:

	Debit	Credit
Cash [asset account]	10,000	
Sales – crops [revenue account]		10,000

Later in the month, the manager sells feeder livestock for $18,000, with final payment to occur at a later date. The resulting journal entry is:

	Debit	Credit
Accounts receivable [asset account]	18,000	
Sales – feeder livestock [revenue account]		18,000

Near the end of the month, the manager sells $2,500 of wool from the farm's herd of sheep, with payment in cash. The resulting journal entry is:

	Debit	Credit
Cash [asset account]	2,500	
Sales – livestock products [revenue account]		2,500

A farm may raise crops that are intended to be fed to livestock, and then the farm manager decides to sell the crops instead. The accounting treatment for these sales is identical to the sales for other types of farm products.

Receipt of Payment from Customers

As we have just noted in several preceding sub-sections, a farm may sell livestock or crops to customers on credit, which means that payment to the farm is delayed. Under these circumstances, an account receivable is recognized as an asset. When the customer eventually pays the farm, the cash receipt offsets the receivable, so that the receivable is eliminated from the accounting records of the farm.

EXAMPLE

A farm manager has sold $4,000 of crops to a neighboring farm, and has secured a promise that payment will be made in 10 days. The initial entry to record the sale is:

	Debit	Credit
Accounts receivable [asset account]	4,000	
Sales – crops [revenue account]		4,000

The payment arrives on time, so the farm accountant records the following entry:

	Debit	Credit
Cash [asset account]	4,000	
Accounts receivable [asset account]		4,000

Crop Insurance Proceeds

Farms routinely pay for crop insurance, which protects them from crop damage, such as from a hail storm. When damage occurs, the farm sends a claim to the insurer. Upon receipt of the insurance proceeds from the insurer, the farm records it as revenue.

EXAMPLE

A farm experiences crop damage from a massive hail storm and submits a claim to its insurer for $43,000. The insurer agrees with the claim and pays the full amount requested. The resulting journal entry is:

	Debit	Credit
Cash [asset account]	43,000	
Crop insurance proceeds [revenue account]		43,000

Summary

The farm accountant will likely deal with the same transactions 90% of the time, or more. To keep from creating any errors when recording these transactions, deal with them the same way, every time. To do so, create a procedure for how to handle the most common recurring transactions. Also, if it is available in the accounting software, create a template for each common transaction, so that the template can be called up and filled in with numbers for the latest transaction. These actions can make the recordation of transactions a smooth and problem-free process.

Chapter 5
Receivables Accounting

Introduction

A farm is not always paid in cash at the point of sale. There are circumstances under which livestock or crops may be sold on credit, which means that payment is expected at a later date. In this case, the farm accountant needs to issue invoices under a billing process through the accounting software, which creates an account receivable. It is possible that some of these receivables will not be paid (called *bad debts*), in which case the accountant needs to account for the related losses. In this chapter, we cover how to engage in a standard billing process to record receivables, and also note the different approaches to recording bad debts.

The Billing Process

When a sale will result in a delayed payment, an invoice must be created that notifies the customer of its liability and when payment is due. The creation of invoices is called the billing process. It involves filling out a form whenever produce is sold and forwarding it to the farm accountant, who creates an invoice for delivery to the customer.

The billing process should be followed every day. Customers are supposed to enter the invoice date in their computer systems when logging in supplier invoices, so that the computer pays each invoice after the correct number of days, as listed in the payment terms on the invoice. However, many accountants do not go to the trouble of entering this date, and instead use the default date, which is the current day. Invoices entered in this manner will be paid later. Thus, it is necessary to process invoices as soon as possible in order to be paid as soon as possible.

The basic billing steps are:

1. Fill out a delivery form when crops or livestock are delivered or shipped to a customer.
2. Forward the completed form to the farm accountant.
3. The farm accountant verifies the sale prices.
4. The farm accountant calculates the amount of shipping to be charged, if any. In many cases, the customer picks up on-site, so there is no delivery charge.
5. The farm accountant loads this information into the billing module of the accounting software and prints two invoices. If applicable, the software may include a sales tax. One copy is sent to the customer, and the other is filed.
6. The software automatically records the sale in the general ledger, which is as follows:

	Debit	Credit
Accounts receivable [asset account]	xxx	
Sales [revenue account]		xxx
Sales tax payable [liability account]		xxx

The Invoice

Accounting software always contains a standard invoice template, which most businesses use with only minor adjustments to bill their customers. The typical invoice contains the following information:

- *Header section.* Itemizes the billing address of the seller and customer, as well as the invoice number, invoice date, and payment due date.
- *Billing detail block.* Lists each item sold to the customer, including the description, unit price, quantity, and extended price.
- *Summary section.* This is an extension of the billing detail block, in which all items sold are summarized. A freight charge and sales tax may be added to arrive at a total invoice amount.

The farm accountant may want to make several modifications to the template to reduce the time required to receive payments from customers, as well as to reduce the number of customer payment errors. Consider implementing the adjustments in the following table.

Invoice Format Changes

Credit card contact information	If customers want to pay with a credit card, include a telephone number to call to pay by this means.
Early payment discount	State the exact amount of the early payment discount and the exact date by which the customer must pay in order to qualify for the discount.
General contact information	If customers have a question about the invoice, there should be a contact information block that states the telephone number and e-mail address they should contact.
Payment due date	Rather than entering payment terms on the invoice (such as "net 30"), state the exact date on which payment is due. This should be stated prominently.

The goal in creating an invoice format is to present the minimum amount of information to the customer in order to prevent confusion, while presenting the required information as clearly as possible. The following sample invoice template incorporates the invoice format changes that we just addressed.

Sample Enhanced Invoice Template

		# Invoice
Customer Address Block	Farm Logo	Shipper Address Block
Invoice Number	Invoice Date	Payment Due Date

Item Description	Unit Quantity	Unit Price	Extended Price

Billing Detail Block

Subtotal	
Freight Charge	
Sales Tax	
Grand Total	

Invoice Problems	Credit Card Payment	Early Payment Discount
Contact Information	Contact Information	Deduct $____ If paid by __/__/__

Cash Sales

Thus far, we have assumed that all sales are made on credit, requiring the issuance of an invoice. It is also possible that a sale transaction will be made in cash, in exchange for the immediate transfer of crops, livestock, or livestock products. This transaction is centered on the cash sale receipt.

A cash sale receipt may look like an invoice, but the intent of the document is entirely different. An invoice is essentially a request to pay as of some future date, while a cash receipt is intended to document what was sold and the amount received in exchange. This document therefore provides proof of purchase to the buyer and proof of cash receipt to the seller.

The cash sale receipt form, which appears in the following exhibit, contains much less information than an invoice. There may be no need to document the name or address of the customer, so this information is excluded. Also, there is no ship-to-address or freight charge, since the customer is presumed to be picking up the purchased goods on the spot. Further, there is no early payment discount information, since payment is at the time of sale. This form is typically filled out manually and in duplicate, with one copy going to the customer and one copy retained for accounting purposes.

Sample Cash Sale Receipt Template

Receipt Number		**Cash Sale Receipt**		
Company Name and Address			Receipt Date	
			Salesperson Name	
Item Description		Unit Quantity	Unit Price	Extended Price
Receipt Detail Block				
			Subtotal	
			Sales Tax	
			Grand Total	

The processing steps for a cash sale are much reduced from those required for an invoice, and are as follows:

1. Enter in the receipt detail block on the cash sale receipt the number of items sold and their prices.
2. Charge sales tax, if applicable.
3. The cash sale receipt is likely a two-part form, so burst the copies apart. Give one copy to the customer and forward one copy to the farm accountant.

4. Record the sale. Use the farm accountant's copy of the cash sale receipt to create a journal entry in the general ledger. The entry will likely be in this format:

	Debit	Credit
Cash [asset account]	xxx	
Sales [revenue account]		xxx
Sales taxes payable [liability account]		xxx

The Accounts Receivable Aging Report

The accounts receivable aging report lists unpaid customer invoices by date ranges. This report is the primary tool used to determine which invoices are overdue for payment. Given its use as a collection tool, the report may be configured to also contain contact information for each customer. The report is also used by the farm manager to determine the effectiveness of collection activities.

A typical aging report lists invoices in 30-day "buckets," where the columns contain the following information:

- The left-most column contains all invoices that are 30 days old or less
- The next column contains invoices that are 31-60 days old
- The next column contains invoices that are 61-90 days old
- The final column contains all older invoices

The report is sorted by customer name, with all invoices for each customer itemized directly below the customer name, usually sorted by either invoice number or invoice date. A sample report follows, though without the individual invoice detail that is usually found in such a report.

Sample Accounts Receivable Aging Report

Customer Name	Total Receivable	0-30 Days	31-60 Days	61-90 Days	90+ Days
Able Granaries	$15,000	$10,000	$5,000		
Bufford Processing	29,000		20,000	$9,000	
Chesterton Co.	83,000	47,000	21,000	12,000	$3,000
Denver Grain Storage	8,000				8,000
Totals	$135,000	$57,000	$46,000	$21,000	$11,000

If the report is generated by an accounting software package, it may be possible to reconfigure the report for different date ranges. For example, if the farm's payment terms are net 15 days, then the date range in the left-most column should only be for the first 15 days. This drops 16-day old invoices into the second column, which highlights that they are now overdue for payment.

Estimation of the Allowance for Doubtful Accounts

The allowance for doubtful accounts is a reduction of the total amount of accounts receivable appearing on a farm's balance sheet, and is listed as a deduction immediately below the accounts receivable line item. Technically, the allowance is called a contra asset account, because it offsets the account with which it is paired, which is accounts receivable.

The allowance for doubtful accounts represents the accountant's best estimate of the amount of accounts receivable that will not be paid by customers. The amount is recognized within the same reporting period as the revenues to which the allowance is related, so that the financial statements reflect all expenses associated with those revenues. The allowance is usually reviewed and updated as part of the month-end closing process, to ensure that the balance is reasonable in comparison to the latest bad debt forecast. For farms having minimal bad debt activity, a quarterly update may be sufficient.

There are several possible ways to estimate the allowance for doubtful accounts, which are:

- *Historical percentage*. If a certain percentage of accounts receivable became bad debts in the past, then use the same percentage in the future to estimate bad debts. This method works best for large numbers of small account balances.
- *Pareto analysis*. Individually review the largest accounts receivable that make up 80% of the total receivable balance, and estimate which specific customers are most likely to default. Then use the preceding historical percentage method for the remaining smaller accounts. This method works best if there are a small number of large account balances.
- *Risk classification*. Assign a risk score to each customer, and assume a higher risk of default for those having a higher risk score.

EXAMPLE

Delgado Ranch periodically obtains new risk scores from a credit agency for all of its customers and loads them into the customer master file. The accounting system's report writing software incorporates this information to create the following report that aggregates the current accounts receivable balance for several categories of risk, to which the historical bad debt percentage for each class of receivables is applied:

Risk Category	Current Receivable Balance	Historical Bad Debt Percentage	Estimated Bad Debt by Risk Category
Low risk	$1,042,500	0.4%	$4,170
Medium low	610,000	1.3%	7,930
Medium high	235,000	3.8%	8,930
High risk	63,000	10.5%	6,615
Totals	$1,950,500	1.4%	$27,645

The result of this largely automated analysis is an estimated bad debt total that can be used to populate the allowance for doubtful accounts.

The accountant can also evaluate the reasonableness of an allowance for doubtful accounts by comparing it to the total amount of seriously overdue accounts receivable, which are presumably not going to be collected. If the allowance is less than the amount of these overdue accounts, the allowance is probably insufficient.

Accounting for the Allowance for Doubtful Accounts

If a farm is using the accrual basis of accounting, the farm accountant should record an allowance for doubtful accounts, which provides an estimate of future bad debts that improves the accuracy of the farm's financial statements. Also, by recording the allowance for doubtful accounts at the same time it records a sale, the farm is properly matching the projected bad debt expense against the related sales item in the same period, which provides an accurate view of the true profitability of a sale.

EXAMPLE

A farm records $1,000,000 of sales to several dozen customers, and projects (based on historical experience) that it will incur 1% of this amount as bad debts, though it does not know exactly which customers will default. It records the 1% of projected bad debts as a $10,000 debit to the bad debt expense account and a $10,000 credit to the allowance for doubtful accounts. The bad debt expense is charged to expense right away, and the allowance for doubtful accounts becomes a reserve account that offsets the account receivable of $1,000,000 (for a net receivable outstanding of $990,000). The entry is:

	Debit	Credit
Bad debt expense [expense account]	10,000	
Allowance for doubtful accounts [asset contra account]		10,000

Later, several customers default on payments totaling $4,000. Accordingly, the farm accountant credits the accounts receivable account by $4,000 to reduce the amount of outstanding accounts receivable and debits the allowance for doubtful accounts by $4,000. This entry reduces the balance in the allowance account to $6,000. The entry does not impact earnings in the current period. The entry is:

	Debit	Credit
Allowance for doubtful accounts [asset contra account]	4,000	
Accounts receivable [asset account]		4,000

A few months later, a collection agency succeeds in collecting $1,500 of the funds that the farm had already written off. The farm accountant can now reverse part of the previous entry, thereby increasing the balances of both accounts receivable and the allowance for doubtful accounts. The entry is:

	Debit	Credit
Accounts receivable [asset account]	1,500	
Allowance for doubtful accounts [asset contra account]		1,500

The only impact that the allowance for doubtful accounts has on the income statement is the initial charge to bad debt expense when the allowance is initially created. Any subsequent write-offs of accounts receivable against the allowance only impact the balance sheet.

The Direct Write-off Method

A less-used method than the allowance method just described is the direct write-off method. The direct write off method is the practice of charging bad debts to expense in the period when individual invoices have been clearly identified as bad debts. The specific activity needed to write off an account receivable under this method is to create a credit memo for the customer in question, which exactly offsets the amount of the bad debt. Creating the credit memo requires a debit to the bad debt expense account and a credit to the accounts receivable account.

This method does not involve a reduction of the amount of recorded sales, only an increase in the bad debt expense. For example, a farm records a sale on credit of $10,000, and records it with a debit to the accounts receivable account and a credit to the sales account. After two months, the customer is only able to pay $8,000 of the open balance, so the farm accountant must write off $2,000. He does so with a $2,000 credit to the accounts receivable account and an offsetting debit to the bad debt expense account. Thus, the revenue amount remains the same, the remaining receivable is eliminated, and an expense is created in the amount of the bad debt.

This approach violates the matching principle, under which all costs related to revenue are charged to expense in the same period in which revenue is recognized, so that the financial results of a farm reveal the entire extent of a revenue-generating transaction in a single accounting period.

The direct write-off method delays the recognition of expenses related to a revenue-generating transaction, making a farm appear more profitable in the short term than it really is. For example, a farm may recognize $10,000 in sales in one period, and then wait three or four months to collect all of the related accounts receivable before finally charging some items off to expense. This creates a lengthy delay between revenue recognition and the recognition of expenses that are directly related to that revenue. Thus, the profit in the initial period is overstated, while profit is understated in the period when the bad debts are charged to expense.

The direct write-off method can be considered a reasonable accounting method if the amount that is written off is an immaterial amount, since doing so has minimal impact on a farm's reported financial results.

The direct write-off method is required for the reporting of taxable income in the United States, since the Internal Revenue Service believes (possibly correctly) that businesses would otherwise be tempted to inflate their bad debt reserves in order to report a smaller amount of taxable income.

Negative Bad Debt Expense

If uncollectible accounts receivable are being written off as they occur (the direct charge-off method), there will be times when a customer unexpectedly pays an invoice after it has been written off. In such a case the write-off should be reversed, which will yield a negative bad debt expense if the original write-off occurred in a reporting period earlier than the reversal. This transaction creates a larger profit in the current income statement, which offsets the lower profit from the previous period in which the bad debt expense was originally recognized.

Conversely, if the accountant is using the allowance method and is charging an estimated amount to bad debt expense each month, an unexpected customer payment against a written-off receivable does not result in the reversal of the original bad debt expense. Instead, the balance in the allowance account is increased by the amount of the unexpected payment. This transaction does not impact the income statement at all; instead, the amount of the allowance is increased in the balance sheet.

Thus, the method used to record bad debts is the key determining factor in whether or not a business can experience a negative bad debt expense.

Summary

When dealing with billings and bad debts, the key factor for the farm accountant is to be very consistent. This means having a clearly-defined process for issuing billings as soon as possible, right after every sale transaction has been completed. Doing so improves the odds of receiving payment sooner. In addition, the accountant must be consistent in the method used to determine the amount of the allowance for doubtful accounts. By doing so, the current allowance should be comparable to the allowance reported in prior periods. It is permissible to change the method used to determine the allowance, but only if doing so results in an improved methodology that will provide better information. Under no circumstances should the method be altered just to provide a short-term boost to reported earnings.

Chapter 6
Investment Accounting

Introduction

There are a number of reasons why a farm might invest in debt and equity securities. The most common reason is that the farm manager is seeking a reasonable return on those excess funds for which there is no immediate operational need. There are specific rules related to the accounting for debt and equity securities, which are addressed in this chapter. These rules are of considerable importance for a farm with significant investments, since they can impact the timing and recognition of investment gains and losses.

Types of Investments

When we refer to investments, we generally mean that a farm has purchased or otherwise acquired securities. A security can be either of the following:

- *Equity security*. This is an ownership position in another business, usually one whose shares are publicly-traded. The common examples of equity securities are common stock and preferred stock. This can also refer to an option or warrant, where the owner has the right, but not the obligation, to purchase the shares of another company.
- *Debt security*. This is a lender relationship where the farm owns a debt instrument, such as a bond, issued by a government or business entity. Examples of debt securities are obligations of the U.S. government, convertible debt, redeemable preferred stock, and commercial paper. The issuer is required to repurchase a debt security on the maturity date of the instrument.

Some types of debt, such as convertible debt, have characteristics of both debt and equity, since there is an option to swap them for equity securities.

Usually, securities can be bought and sold through established exchanges, so they can be easily converted from cash and back into cash within a short period of time. However, some securities may have a more limited market, and so are more difficult to acquire and sell.

EXAMPLE

The farm accountant for Prickly Farms, purveyor of thorn bushes, has $250,000 of excess cash for which there is no immediate need, and decides to invest it. He invests $75,000 in the common stock of Smithy Ironworks. Also, in an effort to avoid paying taxes on interest income, he invests $150,000 in the tax-exempt municipal bonds of the city of Smithville. Finally, he spends $25,000 to acquire warrants that allow the holder to purchase the shares of Nuance Corporation at $12.50 per share, irrespective of the price at which the shares trade.

The common stock and warrants are equity securities, and the municipal bonds are debt securities.

Investment Classifications

When a farm acquires a security, the farm accountant must classify the investment into one of the following three categories:

Investment Classification

Investment Classification	Description	Applies To
Trading securities	This is a security acquired with the intent of selling it in the short-term for a profit.	Debt or equity securities
Held-to-maturity securities	This is a debt security acquired with the intent of holding it to maturity, and where the holder has the ability to do so. This determination should be based not only on intent, but also on a history of being able to do so.	Debt securities
Available-for-sale securities	This is an investment in a security that is not classified as a trading security or a held-to-maturity security. It is not held strictly for short-term profits, nor is it expected to be held to maturity (in the case of debt securities). Thus, it is an "everything else" classification for securities.	Debt or equity securities

Additional points regarding these three investment classifications are as follows:

Trading securities

- *Current asset status.* Since trading securities are expected to be sold in the near term, they are always classified in the balance sheet as current assets. If a security were to be classified as a long-term asset, this would imply that the asset is not a trading security.
- *Fair value requirement.* These securities must have readily determinable fair values. This requirement tends to limit the applicable securities to those registered for trading on an exchange or in the over-the-counter market. If an

investment is in a mutual fund, fair value can be derived from the published fair value of the fund. Securities issued by privately-held entities can be quite difficult to value, and so cannot be considered trading securities, even if the intent is to sell them in the short-term for a profit. Fair value is especially difficult to obtain when there are restrictions on the stock of an investee, since the restrictions limit the ability of the investor to sell the shares.

- *Trading intent*. The intent should be to sell these securities in the short-term for a profit, which can be defined as within the next three months.

Held-to-maturity securities

- *Debt only*. As the title of this security implies, held-to-maturity securities must have maturity dates. Since equity securities do not have maturity dates, they cannot be classified as such.
- *Convertible securities*. A convertible debt security cannot be classified as held-to-maturity, since it is possible that the investor will be tempted to convert the security into the equity of the borrower if the conversion feature is profitable.
- *Collateral status*. A security can be classified as held-to-maturity, even if it is held by a third party as collateral on a loan, as long as the investor expects to repay the underlying borrowing, and so can recover the security.

EXAMPLE

Quest Ranch has invested $250,000 in the debt securities of Pensive Corporation. Since the intent is to hold this debt to its maturity, Quest classifies it as held-to-maturity. Subsequently, Quest uses the securities as collateral on a loan to Farmers Bank. A year later, Quest's financial condition has declined to the point where repayment of the loan is in doubt. Since it is now probable that Quest cannot repay the loan and recover the debt securities, the held-to-maturity classification is no longer appropriate.

- *Intent of the holder*. Use of this classification depends heavily on the intentions of the holder. If there is a reasonable chance that the investor will sell off a debt security as part of its asset management activities, there is no real intent to hold to maturity, and so some other designation must be used. For example, do not use this classification if management is willing to sell a debt security under any of the following circumstances:
    o There are changes in market interest rates
    o There are changes in the prepayment risk associated with a debt security
    o The investor will have a need for liquidity
    o There are changes in the availability of alternative investments
    o There are changes in the available yield on alternative investments

- o There are changes in the sources of available funding, and the terms being offered
- o In response to a tax planning strategy

- *Reclassification policy.* If the investor has a policy of automatically shifting the classification of all held-to-maturity securities to a different classification on a certain date prior to maturity, this implies that the investor never intended to hold any securities to maturity. If so, the held-to-maturity classification should never be used.
- *Borrower deterioration.* It is acceptable to sell a held-to-maturity investment prior to its maturity date if there is an actual deterioration of the creditworthiness of the borrower. However, if the sale occurs prior to the actual deterioration of the creditworthiness of the borrower, this calls into question the intent of the investor to hold its other debt securities through to their maturity dates.
- *Sale prior to maturity date.* It is possible for an investor to sell a held-to-maturity security prior to its maturity date, without interfering with the designation. This can occur in either of the following situations:
  - o The sale is so close to the maturity date that the interest rate risk is essentially eliminated as a factor in the determination of the price of the security; or
  - o The sale occurs after the investor has already collected at least 85% of the outstanding principal.

The general thrust of these additional points for held-to-maturity securities is that the accounting standards are designed to make it quite difficult to use this classification. In most cases, an investor will find that it only uses the trading and available-for-sale classifications for its investments.

Available-for-sale securities

- *Current asset status.* Being an "in between" classification, it is entirely possible that available-for-sale securities will be classified within either current assets or long-term assets on the balance sheet. If the intent is to hold them for less than one year, they should be classified as current assets.

The Realized and Unrealized Gain or Loss

An important concept in the accounting for investments is whether a gain or loss has been realized. A realized gain is achieved by the sale of an investment, as is a realized loss. Conversely, an unrealized gain or loss is associated with a change in the fair value of an investment that is still owned by the investor.

EXAMPLE

Rapunzel Farms owns 500 shares of Tsunami Products common stock. The cost basis of these shares is $10,000, or $20 per share. At the end of the current period, the fair value of the shares has risen by $3, to $23. This translates to a gain of $1,500. Since Rapunzel continues to hold the shares, the gain is unrealized. In the following period, the fair value of the common stock is unchanged. Rapunzel sells the shares, resulting in a realized gain of $1,500.

There are other circumstances than the outright sale of an investment that are considered realized losses. When this happens, a realized loss is recognized in the income statement and the carrying amount of the investment is written down by a corresponding amount. For example, when there is a permanent loss on a held security, the entire amount of the loss is considered a realized loss, and is written off. A permanent loss is typically related to the bankruptcy or liquidity problems of an investee.

EXAMPLE

Langham Ranch invests $100,000 in the common stock of Lethal Sushi. A year later, Lethal files for Chapter 7 liquidation, listing $50 million of liabilities and $32 million of assets. Since common shareholders are paid last, after all creditors and preferred shareholders, it is quite unlikely that Langham will receive any payout. In this situation, and despite still holding the common stock, Langham has experienced a permanent loss, which is considered a realized loss.

Other Comprehensive Income

A term that appears regularly in this chapter is Other Comprehensive Income (OCI). OCI is comprised of those revenues, expenses, gains, and losses that are required by the accounting standards to be excluded from net income on the income statement. This means that they are instead listed after net income on the income statement.

Revenues, expenses, gains, and losses appear in other comprehensive income when they have not yet been realized. The realization concept was noted in an earlier section. For example, if an investor has purchased bonds and the value of those bonds changes, the alteration in value (depending on the circumstances) is recorded as a gain or loss in OCI. When the investor sells the bonds, it realizes a gain or loss on the bonds investment, and can then shift the gain or loss out of other comprehensive income and into a line item higher in the income statement, so that it is part of net income.

EXAMPLE

Treadway Farm buys a bond for $1,000 and classifies it as an available-for-sale security. In the first month, the market value of the bond increases to $1,050, so Treadway records the $50 gain in other comprehensive income. Treadway sells the bond in the second month, and transfers the gain from other comprehensive income to investment income.

OCI is designed to give the reader of a farm's financial statements a more comprehensive view of the financial status of the entity, though in practice it is possible that the concept introduces too much complexity to the income statement. Thus, if a reader does not understand the OCI concept, the recordation of gains and losses and their shifting from OCI to net income may only perplex the person.

An example of the presentation of OCI in the income statement appears next, showing just the relevant line items following the net income line item.

Other Comprehensive Income Example

Net income	$42,000
Other comprehensive income	
Unrealized holding losses on available-for-sale securities	-29,000
Comprehensive income	$13,000

Accumulated other comprehensive income is an account that is classified within the equity section of the balance sheet. It is used to accumulate unrealized gains and losses on those line items in the income statement that are classified within the other comprehensive income category. Once a gain or loss is realized, it is shifted out of the accumulated other comprehensive income account, and instead appears in the retained capital account.

Purchase and Sale of Investments

There are a number of issues that an investor needs to understand that relate to the purchase or sale of investments. In this section, we examine the details of how to calculate a gain or loss on the sale of an investment and other topics related to the purchase and sale of investments.

The Gain or Loss Calculation

At the most basic level, an investor buys an investment and later sells it, hopefully earning a profit from these transactions. What is the accounting for the purchase and sale of an investment? The key points are:

- When buying an investment, the initial cost of the investment is considered to be the purchase price, *plus* any brokerage fees, service fees, and taxes paid.
- When selling an investment, the net proceeds are considered to be the selling price, *minus* any brokerage fees, service fees, and transfer taxes paid.

The difference between these two figures is the realized gain or loss on sale of an investment.

EXAMPLE

Quest Ranch buys 1,000 shares of the common stock of Sharper Designs, at a price of $18.50 per share. Quest also incurs a $75 brokerage fee. Thus, the total cost of the investment is $18,575. The calculation is:

(1,000 Shares × $18.50/share) + $75 Brokerage fee

One year later, Quest sells all 1,000 shares for $19.25, while also incurring another $75 brokerage fee and also paying $150 in transfer taxes. Thus, the total proceeds from the sale are $19,025. The calculation is:

(1,000 Shares × $19.25/share) - $75 Brokerage fee - $150 Transfer taxes

Quest's capital gain on this investment transaction is $450, which is calculated as the net proceeds of $19,025, minus the adjusted cost basis of $18,575.

Conversion of Securities

There are situations in which an investor may hold a convertible security, such as a convertible bond or convertible preferred stock. The conversion feature allows an investor to convert the security into the common stock of the issuer, using a pre-determined conversion ratio. This conversion feature is valuable to an investor, who is protected against a decline in his investment by the interest payments made on the security (if the security is convertible debt), while also retaining the upside potential of an increase in the price of the common stock into which the security can be converted. If the price of the issuing entity's common stock does not increase, the investor does not convert its holdings into common stock, and instead continues to receive interest payments.

Since the only reason to convert to the common stock of the issuer is to take advantage of a price increase in the common stock, there should always be a gain when this conversion occurs. The investor records the market value of the common stock that it receives from the conversion. The difference between the cost basis of the security given up and the market value of the replacement stock is recognized as a gain in the investor's income statement.

EXAMPLE

Hanson Farms owns 800 convertible bonds issued by Horton Corporation. The terms of the bonds state that they can be converted into ten shares of Horton's common stock, beginning five years after the issuance date of the bonds. Following the designated waiting period, Hanson's accountant notes that the bonds have a market value of $800,000, while the amount of common stock into which the bonds could be converted has a market value of $845,000. The accountant therefore converts of the bonds and records the following transaction:

	Debit	Credit
Investments – Equity securities [asset account]	845,000	
Investments – Convertible bonds [asset account]		800,000
Gain on bond conversion [gain/loss account]		45,000

Sale of Securities

The basic transaction to record the sale of an investment is to debit the cash account and credit the investment account, thereby eliminating the investment from the balance sheet. There are two alternatives for how to deal with gains or losses associated with these investments, which are:

- *Realized gains and losses.* If an investment is classified as a trading security, any gains and losses associated with changes in its fair value have been recognized in earnings at the end of each reporting period, so there may be no gain or loss left to recognize. The only possible gain or loss will have arisen between the end of the last reporting period and the sale date.
- *Unrealized gains and losses.* If an investment is classified as available-for-sale, any unrealized holding gains and losses associated with changes in its fair value have been recognized in other comprehensive income. As of the sale date, shift these gains and losses from other comprehensive income to earnings.

Accounting for Dividends and Interest Income

Thus far, we have been solely concerned with the purchase and sale of investments. But what about the more mundane receipt of dividends and interest income from those investments? The accounting for these items is relatively simple. In both cases, it is recorded as a component of other income. This means it is not considered part of the revenue of the investor, but is instead recorded in a line item lower down in the income statement. The following example shows the flow of transactions required to account for these items.

EXAMPLE

Nonesuch Farms has purchased 2,000 shares of the common stock of Mulligan Imports. Mulligan's board of directors declares an annual dividend of $1.00 at its March board meeting, to be paid in May. Nonesuch's accountant is informed of the dividend declaration, and records the following receivable in March:

	Debit	Credit
Dividends receivable [asset account]	2,000	
Other income – dividends [other income account]		2,000

Mulligan pays the dividend in May. Upon receipt of the cash, Nonesuch's accountant records the following entry:

	Debit	Credit
Cash [asset account]	2,000	
Dividends receivable [asset account]		2,000

Nonesuch also bought $20,000 of the bonds of Spud Potato Farms at their face value. There is no discount or premium to be amortized. Spud pays 7% interest on these bonds at the end of each year. Upon receipt of the payment, the accountant records the following transaction:

	Debit	Credit
Cash [asset account]	1,400	
Other income – interest [other income account]		1,400

Stock Dividends and Stock Splits

An issuer of equity securities may issue additional shares to its investors, which is called a stock dividend. Investors do not pay extra for these shares, so there is no need to record an accounting transaction. The only change from the perspective of the investor is that the cost basis per share has now declined, since the carrying amount of the investment is being spread over more shares.

EXAMPLE

Colton Farm owns 10,000 shares of Kelvin Corporation, for which the carrying amount on Colton's books is $124,000. At the end of the year, Kelvin's board of directors elects to issue a stock dividend to investors at a ratio of one additional share for every ten shares owned. This means that Colton receives an additional 1,000 shares of Kelvin. The issuance of the stock dividend alters Colton's cost basis in the stock as follows:

	Shares Held	Carrying Amount	Cost Basis per Share
Before stock dividend	10,000	$124,000	$12.40
After stock dividend	11,000	124,000	$11.27

An issuer may also conduct a stock split, where more than 20% to 25% of the shares outstanding prior to the issuance are issued to existing shareholders. Though the issuer is required to account for this transaction, the number of shares issued has no impact on the investor, who still has no accounting entry to make – there is just a reduction in the cost basis per share, as just noted for a stock dividend.

Ongoing Accounting for Investments

When a farm acquires debt or equity securities for investment purposes, it must be cognizant of how these investments are to be classified, since the classification drives the accounting treatment. The following table summarizes the initial and subsequent accounting for the three classifications of investments.

Investment Accounting Table

Investment Type	Initial Recordation	Subsequent Accounting
Trading securities	Initially record at the purchase cost of the securities.	Measure at their fair value on the balance sheet, and include all unrealized holding gains and losses in earnings. Evidence of fair value can be obtained from the market prices at which these securities are selling on each measurement date.
Held-to-maturity securities	Initially record at the purchase cost of the securities.	Measure all held-to-maturity debt securities at their amortized cost in the balance sheet. Thus, there is no adjustment to fair value.
Available-for-sale securities	Initially record at the purchase cost of the securities.	Measure available-for-sale securities at their fair value on the balance sheet, and include all unrealized holding gains and losses in other comprehensive income until realized (i.e., when the securities are sold).

For all three investment types, when an investment is sold (i.e., realized) recognize the resulting gain or loss in the income statement. A gain or loss resulting from a sale does not appear in other comprehensive income.

EXAMPLE

Armadillo Ranch buys $150,000 of equity securities that it classifies as available-for-sale. After six months pass, the quoted market price of these securities declines to $130,000. Armadillo records the decline in value with the following entry:

	Debit	Credit
Loss on available-for-sale securities (recorded in other comprehensive income) [gain/loss account]	20,000	
Investments – Available-for-sale [asset account]		20,000

Three months later, the securities have regained $6,000 of value, which results in the following entry:

	Debit	Credit
Investments – Available-for-sale [asset account]	6,000	
Gain on available-for-sale securities (recorded in other comprehensive income) [gain/loss account]		6,000

A key difference from the accounting noted in the preceding Investment Accounting Table is that the holder of certain securities has the option to measure those securities at their fair value. If the investor elects to take this option, it will compile unrealized gains and losses in the same manner used for available-for-sale investments. The following section clarifies this option.

The Fair Value Option

A business has the option to record its available-for-sale and held-for-sale investments at their fair values, which is called the fair value option. GAAP allows this option under the theory that doing so gives users a better assessment of the current valuation of an organization's assets. The net effect of taking this option is that the unrealized gains and losses associated with available-for-sale and held-for-sale investments are recognized in earnings on each subsequent reporting date, rather than in other comprehensive income.

If the farm manager elects to measure investments at their fair value, do so on an instrument-by-instrument basis. Once the election has been made to follow the fair value option for an instrument, the change in reporting is irrevocable. In most cases, it is acceptable to choose the fair value option for an eligible item while not electing to use it for other items that are essentially identical.

Summary

The accounting for the three types of investments clearly differs, and so it would initially appear that a considerable amount of detailed investment monitoring is required to ensure that the related accounting will be correct. However, the situation can be made less complex as long as a clear procedure is developed for the treatment of each class of investment. The situation can be further clarified by restricting all investments to just one or two of the three allowed classifications (such as not using the held-to-maturity classification). Following these rules can result in greatly simplified accounting for debt and equity investments.

Chapter 7
Inventory Accounting

Introduction

In agricultural accounting, one of the most critical areas is the accounting for inventory. Inventory is an asset that is intended to be sold or used in the ordinary course of business. Inventory items can fall into one of the following three categories:

- Held for sale in the ordinary course of business; or
- That is in the process of being produced for sale; or
- The materials or supplies intended for consumption in the production process.

An example of inventory that is held for sale is raised crops that will be sold. An example of inventory in the process of being produced for sale is raised livestock that are intended for sale. Finally, an example of supplies intended for consumption in the production process is purchased feed.

The general rule for valuing agricultural inventory is to do so at the lower of cost or market, which is the standard GAAP pronouncement for most industries. However, this rule does not hold true in all situations, as we will see in the following discussion. In certain cases, inventory can be valued at net realizable value.

Accounting for Inventory – at Period-end

Under the accrual basis of accounting, the costs of raising or purchasing inventory are recorded as an asset when costs are incurred for them. At the end of the reporting period, the remaining amount of inventory is tallied and then subtracted from the amount of inventory stated in the accounting records to arrive at the amount of inventory that will be charged to expense. This is called the *periodic* inventory system.

EXAMPLE

A farm has a beginning inventory balance of $150,000. During the year, the farm incurs $525,000 of inventory-related costs. At the end of the year, the amount of inventory remaining on hand is verified, and it is determined that the ending inventory valuation is $115,000. Based on this information, the calculation of the amount of inventory to charge to expense within the year is:

Beginning inventory	+$150,000
+ Additions to inventory	+ 525,000
- Ending inventory	- 115,000
= Inventory charged to expense	$560,000

The ending inventory balance of $115,000 appears in the farm's year-end balance sheet, while the $560,000 charged to expense appears in its income statement.

Under the periodic system, the easiest way to compile costs is to record them directly into the inventory account for each asset type, and then reduce the resulting balance at the end of the reporting period to match the value of the actual on-hand inventory.

The periodic inventory system is easy to use, but suffers from one key problem, which is that the inventory must be physically counted whenever financial statements are needed, in order to determine how much of the inventory to charge to expense. Doing so at the end of the year is the absolute minimum that a farm manager should allow, since the financial performance of the farm is in doubt for the other 11 months. A better approach is to conduct an inventory count at the end of each quarter. Another possibility is to conduct a rough count at the end of each month and a more detailed count at the end of each quarter, so that financial statements can be produced that give a fair representation of the performance of the farm.

The form in the following exhibit can be used to manually record the period-end inventory of crops. Some variation on this form should be used every time an inventory count is conducted, to ensure that the same calculation process is used; this results in more consistent counts.

Sample Crop Ending Inventory Form

	Quantity	Price	Total Value
Corn		$	$
Soybeans			
Hay, alfalfa			
Hay, other			
Oats			
Silage			
Straw			
Wheat			
Other grains			
		Total crops	$

Along the same lines, the forms in the following three exhibits can be used to manually record the period-end inventory of beef cattle, dairy cattle, and hogs.

Sample Beef Cattle Inventory Form

	Quantity	Price	Total Value
Cows		$	$
Bred heifers			
Heifer calves			
Bulls			
Total breeding stock			$
Calves			
Yearlings			
Total market cattle			$

Sample Dairy Cattle Inventory Form

	Quantity	Price	Total Value
Cows		$	$
Bred heifers			
Heifer calves			
Bulls			
Total breeding stock			$
Calves			
Yearlings			
Total market cattle			$

Sample Hog Inventory Form

	Quantity	Price	Total Value
Sows		$	$
Gilts			
Boars			
Total breeding stock			$
Market hogs			
Feeder pigs			
Nursery pigs			
Total market hogs			$

Similarly, the form in the following exhibit can be used to manually record the period-end inventory of supplies.

Sample Supplies Ending Inventory Form

	Quantity	Price	Total Value
Commercial feed		$	$
Fertilizer			
Fuel			
Livestock products			
Pesticides			
Seed			
		Total supplies	$

At a more simplistic level, it will likely be useful to maintain an ongoing record of livestock quantities, average weights, and values, as noted in the following exhibit.

Livestock Record

Year:		Start Date			End of Year		
#	Livestock Type	Qty	Ave. Weight	Value	Qty	Ave. Weight	Value
1							
2							
3							
4							
5							
6							
7							
8							

Summary of Inventory Valuation Rules

Agricultural inventory is subject to a number of classification and valuation alternatives, of which the farm accountant should be aware. In the following exhibit, we note the different classifications that can be applied to each type of inventory for accounting purposes. A different account could be set up to track the costs within each of these classifications.

Inventory Classifications

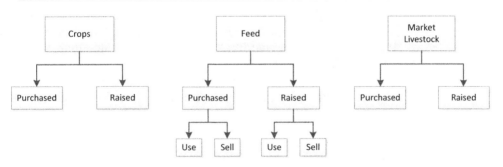

A different classification scheme is used when determining how to value inventory. From a valuation perspective, the key element is whether the inventory was purchased or raised, after which the intended use of the inventory is considered. The classification scheme from a valuation viewpoint appears in the following exhibit.

Classifications for Valuation Purposes

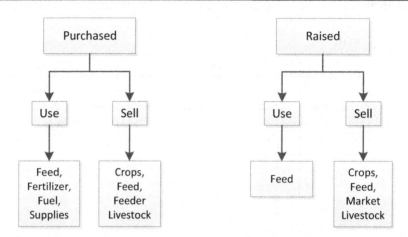

The baseline GAAP position is that inventory is to be valued at the lower of its cost or market; this usually means that inventory is to be valued at its cost. However, GAAP also allows under certain circumstances that net realizable value can be used to value crops and market livestock. *Net realizable value* is the estimated selling price of something in the ordinary course of business, with deductions for costs of completion, disposal, and transport.

We note in the following bullet points the accounting treatment for each of the classifications used for valuation purposes, as noted in the preceding exhibit:

- Inventory purchased for use

  o Includes feed, fertilizer, fuel, and supplies
  o Value at cost

- Inventory purchased for sale

  o Includes crops, feed, and livestock intended for sale after a feeding period (feeder livestock)
  o Value at the lower of the original cost or the current market value
  o Net realizable value can be used when the preceding valuation options are not available
  o Do not use the net realizable value option for feed

- Inventory raised for use

  o Includes feed intended for feeding animals
  o Value the inventory at the lower of the actual cost to produce it or the cost at which it could currently be purchased on the market
  o Valuation at net realizable value is not allowed

- Inventory raised for sale
  - o Includes crops, feed intended for sale, and livestock intended for sale (market livestock)
  - o The actual cost of raising inventory is difficult to determine, but can be used to value the inventory
  - o If the actual cost of raising inventory is too difficult, net realizable value can be used

Clearly, there are a number of valuation issues to be aware of when dealing with inventory. The most critical of these issues is whether the net realizable value option is used. When there is a valuation adjustment for net realizable value, the amount of the adjustment appears in the income statement as a revision of the revenue line item. Thus, a change in the valuation of inventory can alter farm revenues, even though a sale has not yet been made. This accounting treatment is used because net realizable value is based on the sales that would be generated if the inventory were to be sold. Logically, then, a change in inventory valuation should alter the amount of recognized revenue.

EXAMPLE

Monroe Farms has just harvested a crop of corn. The intent is to sell the corn. The corn can be valued at its net realizable value.

Jackson Ranch has harvested a field of hay. The intent is to use the hay to feed the ranch's livestock. The farm does not track the cost associated with growing and harvesting the hay, so the accountant must value the hay at the price the ranch would pay if it had to buy the hay on the open market.

Adams Ranch has purchased feed. The intent is to use the feed in the ranch's feedlot operations. This is inventory purchased for use, so it must be valued at the purchase cost of the feed.

Polk Farm has purchased feeder hogs. The intent is to feed the hogs in the farm's feedlot operations and then sell the hogs. This is inventory purchased for sale, so it should be valued at the lower of the original cost or the current market value. The original cost was $525 per hog and the current market value is $630, so the accountant must value the hogs at $525 each.

We expand upon these summary rules in the following sections.

Accounting for Inventory - Feed

In the following sub-sections, we note the accounting for three different situations involving feed – when it is purchased for internal use, when it is purchased for resale, and when it is raised for internal use.

Purchase of Feed for Internal Use

When feed is purchased for internal use, the purchase is recorded in the most relevant inventory account. The number of feed accounts used will depend on the level of precision that the farm manager wants to achieve in tracking costs. A single inventory account could be used, such as Inventory – Feed. Or, there could be a separate account for each type of feed, such as:

- Inventory – Feed – Hay
- Inventory – Feed – Hay Cubes
- Inventory – Feed – Pellets
- Inventory – Feed – Purchased Grain
- Inventory – Feed – Salt and Mineral Supplements

In the preceding list, we standardize the use of "Inventory" and "Feed" so that these types of inventory can be clustered together in the chart of accounts. The specific identification of the type of feed is then stated in the third information block.

There is no ideal amount of tracking required for the costs of feed. If an additional account is created and no one makes use of the resulting information, then that account was not needed. This advice extends to all types of inventory.

The accounting for purchased feed is relatively easy, since there are cost records from when the purchases were made, and this type of inventory tends to turn over (be consumed) relatively quickly, making for relatively low inventory levels to count. The accounting steps are:

1. Record all purchases in the most applicable feed inventory account.
2. Count the amount of purchased feed on hand at the end of the reporting period.
3. Conduct the periodic inventory calculation already noted to derive the amount of inventory to charge to expense.
4. Record the expense charge with a journal entry.

EXAMPLE

A farm has a beginning balance of $500 of hay cubes in the first quarter of the year. The farm purchases another $3,500 of hay cubes during the quarter. These purchases are recorded in the Inventory – Feed – Hay Cubes account. At the end of the quarter, the farm manager counts $800 of hay cubes still on the premises, so $3,200 of hay cubes were consumed during the quarter. The calculation is:

$500 Beginning inventory + $3,500 Purchases - $800 Ending inventory = $3,200 Usage

The farm accountant then records the following entry to shift the $3,200 of usage from the inventory asset to an expense account:

	Debit	Credit
Purchased feed [expense account]	3,200	
Inventory – feed – hay cubes [asset account]		3,200

The journal entry in the preceding example shows that a certain amount of the inventory asset has been consumed, which appears in the income statement as an expense.

Purchase of Feed for Resale

A farm manager could elect to purchase feed with the intent of reselling it at a later date. If so, the accounting is exactly the same as was just described for the purchase of feed for internal use. The only difference is if the farm manager wants to understand the performance of these purchase-and-resale transactions. When this is the case, purchases of feed intended for resale can be recorded in a separate inventory account such as Inventory – Feed Purchased for Resale. At the end of the reporting period, the amount in this account that is to be charged to expense can be charged to a distinct expense account, such as Purchased Feed for Resale.

As usual, this distinction is not necessary if the resulting information will not be used.

EXAMPLE

A farm manager occasionally buys and resells grain that is intended for feed purposes; he is speculating that the price of the feed will increase during the holding period. Since he wants to judge the performance of his speculation activities, he records these purchases in a separate account. In the most recent period, the amount of beginning inventory for purchased feed intended for resale was $8,300. An additional $2,700 of grain was purchased during the period, and the ending inventory balance was $6,500. This resulted in a charge to expense of $4,500, for which the calculation is:

$8,300 Beginning inventory + $2,700 Purchases - $6,500 Ending inventory = $4,500 Usage

The farm accountant then records the following entry to shift the $4,500 of usage from the inventory asset to an expense account:

	Debit	Credit
Purchased feed for resale [expense account]	4,500	
Inventory – feed purchased for resale [asset account]		4,500

Raised Feed for Internal Use

A farm may raise feed for use within its own operations. This feed has a market value (the cost at which it could currently be purchased on the market), which can be assigned to the inventory and also recorded as a change in revenue in the income statement. At the end of the reporting period, the amount of raised feed is determined and valued based on the market price at the end of the period. This ending valuation is then compared to the valuation already in the relevant inventory account from the beginning of the reporting period; the difference is recorded in a revenue account. Over time, the balance in the inventory account will fluctuate as the feed is used up internally; this will result in increases and decreases in the amount of revenue attributable to the feed. If all of the feed is eventually used internally, then the net effect on revenue over time will be zero.

Though the market value approach is possible, the preferred approach is to value feed raised for internal use at the lower of cost or market. Doing so avoids the recognition (and possible later reduction) of revenue that can occur as feed stocks rise and fall.

If the amount of feed raised for internal use is minor, and especially if the amount raised has been consumed by the end of the year, it is possible to simply not record any transactions, since there will be no impact on the financial statements as of the end of the year.

If the farm manager wants to track raised feed for internal use, then a separate inventory account will be needed for it, such as Inventory – Feed Raised for Use.

Accounting for Inventory – Crops

In the following sub-sections, we note the accounting for crops under three scenarios – when crops have been purchased for resale, when crops are still growing, and when crops have been raised for sale.

Purchase of Crops for Resale

When crops are purchased for resale, the farm manager may want to track the success of these transactions. If so, the purchases should be recorded in a separate inventory account, such as Inventory – Crops Purchased for Resale. At the end of the reporting period, the usual periodic inventory calculation is conducted, and the amount of purchased crops to be charged to expense is charged to a distinct expense account, such as Purchased Crops for Resale.

EXAMPLE

A farm manager sometimes buys and resells crops, in hopes of earning a profit from expected increases in the market price of the crops. In order to review the results of these speculative activities, he records the purchases in a separate account. In the most recent period, the amount of beginning inventory for purchased crops intended for resale was $1,000. An additional $14,250 was purchased during the period, and the ending inventory balance was $8,900. This results in a charge to expense of $6,350, for which the calculation is:

$1,000 Beginning inventory + $14,250 Purchases - $8,900 Ending inventory = $6,350 Usage

The farm accountant then records the following entry to shift the $6,350 of usage from the inventory asset to an expense account:

	Debit	Credit
Purchased crops for resale [expense account]	6,350	
Inventory – crops purchased for resale [asset account]		6,350

Growing Crops

Field and row crops are typically planted from seeds or transplanted from beds, and then developed to the point of harvesting within a period of months. When these crops have a cycle of less than one year, they are referred to as *annuals*. Examples of these crops are noted in the following exhibit.

Sample Annual Crops

Barley	Crops raised for seed	Soybeans
Beans	Lettuce	Sugar beets
Cabbage	Melons	Tobacco
Corn	Milo	Tomatoes
Cotton		Wheat

All costs of growing crops are to be accumulated until harvesting time. This rule includes crop costs that are incurred before planting, such as the cost of soil preparation.

Some costs associated with growing crops are not incurred until after the harvest, perhaps not until the next year. For example, there may be a residue of harvested crops in the fields that is not cleared until the start of the next growing season. These costs should be accrued and allocated to the harvested crop.

The cost of growing crops should be reported at the lower of cost or market. Once crops have been raised, the rules in the following sub-section apply, which include the prospect of valuing the inventory at its net realizable value.

Raised Crops for Sale

A farm may raise crops for sale and store those crops prior to their eventual sale. The farm accountant can assign actual costs to these crops, though the cost accumulation process can be difficult. Another way to value raised crops is to do so at their selling price, less any estimated costs of disposal. This net realizable value option is only available if all of the following conditions are present:

- The product is available for immediate delivery
- The costs of disposal are predictable and insignificant
- The product has a readily determinable and reliable market price

When net realizable value is assigned to the inventory, it is also recorded as a change in revenue in the income statement. At the end of the reporting period, the amount of raised crops is determined and valued based on the net realizable value at the end of the period. This ending valuation is then compared to the valuation already in the relevant inventory account from the beginning of the reporting period; the difference is recorded in a revenue account.

The net realizable value of the raised crops is recorded in an inventory account. For example, it could be named Inventory – Crops Raised for Sale. Changes in the balance in this account are recorded in a revenue account, such as Change in Value of Crop Inventory.

EXAMPLE

A farm raises wheat as its principal crop. One field has just been harvested, and the market value of that wheat is $42,000. The farm manager believes that the market price of wheat will increase, so he elects to only sell $10,000 of the crop at once, which is a cash sale. The journal entry for that transaction is:

	Debit	Credit
Cash [asset account]	10,000	
Sales – crops [revenue account]		10,000

The remainder of the crop, having a market value of $32,000, is placed in storage. This results in the following journal entry:

	Debit	Credit
Inventory – crops raised for use [asset account]	32,000	
Change in value of crop inventory [revenue account]		32,000

The result is an immediate increase in revenue of $42,000, where $10,000 comes from a cash sale and the remainder from the market value of the remaining crops.

One month later, the farm manager finds that he guessed wrong about the direction of wheat prices when he finds that the market value of his stored crop has now declined by $1,000, from

$32,000 to $31,000. This results in the following journal entry, which reduces the value of the crop asset and the amount of recognized revenue:

	Debit	Credit
Change in value of crop inventory [revenue account]	1,000	
Inventory – crops raised for use [asset account]		1,000

Accounting for Inventory - Livestock

Any animal that has a short productive life is classified as inventory. Poultry is an example. This means that the cost of flocks can be classified as inventory.

The following sub-sections deal with the accounting for three situations involving livestock – when livestock has been purchased for resale, when livestock has been raised for sale, and the treatment of livestock products.

Purchase of Market Livestock for Resale

A farm manager may elect to buy market livestock with the intent of reselling it at a later date. The cost of these purchases can be recorded in a general account, such as Inventory – Feeder Livestock. However, that account includes both raised and purchased livestock. If the farm manager wants to track the success of the purchase and resale transactions, the purchases should instead be recorded in a more targeted account, such as Inventory – Feeder Livestock Purchased for Resale. At the end of the reporting period, the usual periodic inventory calculation is conducted, and the amount of purchased market livestock to be charged to expense is charged to a distinct expense account, such as Feeder Livestock.

EXAMPLE

A farm manager buys 10 sheep for $3,500, with the intent of selling them later in the season. This results in the following entry:

	Debit	Credit
Feeder livestock purchased for resale [asset account]	3,500	
Cash [asset account]		3,500

There was no beginning inventory of sheep intended for resale. At the end of the year, there are only three sheep left. Their cost is 30% of the original cost, since the other 70% of the sheep have been sold. This means the inventory account balance should be reduced to $1,050, which is accomplished with the following entry:

	Debit	Credit
Feeder livestock [expense account]	2,450	
Feeder livestock purchased for resale [asset account]		2,450

Raised Market Livestock for Sale

A farm may raise livestock for sale. When animals are available and held for sale, the farm accountant can value the livestock at their selling price, less any estimated costs of disposal. This net realizable value option is only available if all of the following conditions are present:

- There are reliable and realizable market prices for the animals, which are readily determinable
- Disposal costs are insignificant and predictable
- The animals are available for immediate delivery

The livestock has a market value, which is assigned to the inventory and also recorded as a change in revenue in the income statement. At the end of the reporting period, the amount of raised livestock is determined and valued based on the market price at the end of the period. This ending valuation is then compared to the valuation already in the relevant inventory account from the beginning of the reporting period; the difference is recorded in a revenue account.

It is not always easy to determine the value of livestock. One approach for the farm accountant is to use a reputable outside source for this information. These values are estimates, which are based on the following factors:

- *The age of the livestock.* The value of animals changes as they progress through the various age groups while they remain in a herd or flock.
- *The value of each age group.* The estimated value of each age group may change over time.

The value of the raised market livestock is recorded in an inventory account. For example, it could be named Inventory – Feeder Livestock Raised for Sale. Changes in the balance in this account are recorded in a revenue account, such as Change in Value of Raised Feeder Livestock.

EXAMPLE

A farm raises pigs as feeder livestock, which it intends to sell. At the end of the current reporting period, the farm accountant tallies the number of feeder pigs, and notes that there are 2,413
pigs. At the current market price, these pigs have a value of $543,000. The beginning balance
of feeder pigs raised for sale was $489,000, so there has been an increase of $54,000 in the
value of the farm's feeder livestock. This results in the following journal entry:

	Debit	Credit
Inventory – feeder livestock raised for sale [asset account]	54,000	
Change in value of raised feeder livestock [revenue account]		54,000

Livestock Products

There may be instances in which a production animal produces more than one product.
For example:

- Sheep can produce lambs, wool, and meat
- Dairy cattle can produce milk, calves, and meat

In the examples, lambs and milk are (respectively) likely to be the primary products.
Secondary products are likely to be wool and calves. In these cases, costs are allocated
to the primary and secondary products based on their relative values. If meat is produced, it is typically considered to be a residual byproduct. The exact method used for
allocating costs will depend on the breeding, production, and marketing practices of
the farm.

Inventory Co-Mingling

In addition to the valuation rules just noted, the farm accountant must also be aware
of the problems that can arise when inventory items having different values are co-
mingled. For example, feed may be purchased at one price on Monday and then purchased again on Wednesday at a different price. Since the feed is likely mixed together
in a single storage location, the accountant must now deal with inventory that was
acquired at different prices, but which cannot be separately identified. This issue is
dealt with using the weighted-average method.

   When using the weighted average method, divide the cost of goods available for
sale by the number of units available for sale, which yields the weighted-average cost
per unit. In this calculation, the cost of goods available for sale is the sum of beginning
inventory and net purchases. This weighted-average figure is then used to assign a
cost to both ending inventory and the cost of goods sold.

EXAMPLE

The farm accountant for Milton Acres Ranch elects to use the weighted-average method for the month of May for the purchase and sale of hogs. During that month, he records the following transactions:

	Quantity Change	Actual Unit Cost	Actual Total Cost
Beginning inventory	+150	$220	$33,000
Sale	-125		
Purchase	+200	270	54,000
Sale	-150		
Purchase	+100	290	29,000
Ending inventory	= 175		$116,000

The actual total cost of all purchased or beginning inventory hogs in the preceding table is $116,000 ($33,000 + $54,000 + $29,000). The total of all purchased or beginning inventory hogs is 450 (150 beginning inventory + 300 purchased). The weighted average cost per hog is therefore $257.78 ($116,000 ÷ 450 hogs).

The ending inventory valuation is $45,112 (175 hogs × $257.78 weighted average cost), while the cost of goods sold valuation is $70,890 (275 hogs × $257.78 weighted average cost). The sum of these two amounts (less a rounding error) equals the $116,000 total actual cost of all purchases and beginning inventory.

It is also possible that purchased and raised inventory is co-mingled. There is no GAAP guidance for how to deal with this situation. The Farm Financial Standards Council recommends that the farm accountant make an assumption that all inventory items on hand at the end of the reporting period were purchased. By using this assumption, one can then construct the following rules for valuing inventory:

- If the amount of inventory purchased ends up being greater than the amount on hand at the end of the reporting period, then use the weighted-average purchase cost or the current market value to value the inventory.
- If the amount of inventory purchased ends up being less than the amount on hand, then only value the number of purchased items at the weighted-average purchase cost. The residual inventory is assumed to have been raised; this amount is valued based on the applicable method, as outlined earlier in the chapter.

EXAMPLE

White Star Ranch had 25 raised feeder hogs on hand at the beginning of March, when it purchased an additional 40 hogs, for a total of 65 hogs. The 40 hogs are valued at their weighted-average purchase price of $290 each, while the 25 raised hogs are valued at their net realizable values.

If White Star were to sell 30 hogs by the end of the year, all of the raised hogs are assumed to have been sold. The remaining 35 hogs are all valued at the $290 weighted-average cost.

If White Star were to sell just 10 hogs by the end of the year, there would still be 55 left. Ten raised hogs are assumed to have been sold, so 15 hogs are valued at their net realizable value and 40 are valued at the $290 weighted-average cost.

Summary

GAAP is generally quite clear about only valuing any kind of inventory at the lower of cost or market. However, the *AICPA Audit and Accounting Guide* notes that agricultural producers can avoid a cost-based valuation and instead use net realizable value, but only under circumstances where market prices are clearly available, disposal costs are minor, and the products are available for immediate sale. These special conditions appear to have been crafted specifically for farmers, since they are applicable in many situations. The main categories of inventory to which net realizable value cannot be applied are developing crops and livestock, as well as specialty crops that may have uncertain demand and therefore an uncertain price. The farm accountant must be quite clear about the classification of farm inventory, so that net realizable value is only used for the allowed classifications.

Chapter 8
Fixed Assets and Depreciation

Introduction

A farm will likely need to invest in a number of expensive assets in order to have adequate facilities and properly handle livestock and crops. These assets are called fixed assets, and are accounted for quite differently from most types of farm expenditures. In this chapter, we describe fixed assets, how they are measured, and the options for depreciating them, as well as several related topics.

> **Related Podcast Episodes:** Episodes 15, 109, 122, 139, and 196 of the Accounting Best Practices Podcast discuss various aspects of fixed asset accounting. They are available at: **accountingtools.com/podcasts** or **iTunes**

The Nature of Fixed Assets

A farm manager may invest in a variety of fixed assets. A fixed asset is an item with a useful life expected to exceed one reporting period, and costing more than a minimum threshold known as the capitalization limit. The *capitalization limit* is the amount paid for an asset, above which a farm records it as a fixed asset. If the farm pays less than the capitalization limit for an asset, it charges the asset to expense in the period incurred. This limit is imposed in order to reduce the record keeping associated with longer-term assets.

By designating an expenditure as a fixed asset, the expenditure is shifted away from the income statement, where expenditures normally go, and instead is placed in the balance sheet. As we gradually reduce its recorded cost through depreciation (as discussed in a later section), the expenditure flows from the balance sheet to the income statement. Thus, the main difference between a normal expenditure and a fixed asset is that the fixed asset is charged to expense over a longer period of time.

A fixed asset is not purchased or constructed with the intent of immediate resale, but rather for productive use within the farm. The following are examples of general categories of fixed assets:

- Buildings
- Computer equipment and software
- Intangible assets
- Land
- Office furniture and equipment
- Perennial crops
- Purchased breeding livestock

- Tractors
- Vehicles

Farm equipment may be manually tracked within an equipment inventory record, such as the one appearing in the following table.

Farm Equipment Record

#	Item Description	Serial No.	Model	Asset Category	Location	Purchase Date	Cost
1							
2							
3							
4							
5							
6							
7							
8							

It may also be useful to maintain an equipment repair log, in which can be recorded the repair details for each separate repair event.

Equipment Repair Log

Date		Model	
Equipment		Serial Number	
Repair details | cost			
Repaired by		**Warranty:** Yes | No	
Parts replaced			

Fixed assets are initially recorded as assets, and are then subject to the following general types of accounting transactions:

- Periodic depreciation
- Impairment write-downs
- Disposition

All three of these transactions are discussed in the following sections.

A fixed asset appears in the financial records at its *net book value* (also known as its carrying amount or carrying value), which is its original cost, minus accumulated depreciation, minus any impairment charges. Because of ongoing depreciation, the net book value of a fixed asset is always declining.

The Initial Measurement of a Fixed Asset

Initially record a fixed asset at the historical cost of acquiring it, which includes the costs to bring it to the condition and location necessary for its intended use. If these preparatory activities will occupy a period of time, also include in the cost of the asset the interest costs related to the cost of the asset during the preparation period.

The activities involved in bringing a fixed asset to the condition and location necessary for its intended purpose include the following:

- Physical construction of the asset
- Demolition of any preexisting structures
- Renovating a preexisting structure to alter it for use by the buyer
- Administrative and technical activities during preconstruction for such activities as designing the asset and obtaining permits
- Administrative and technical work after construction commences for such activities as litigation, labor disputes, and technical problems

---

EXAMPLE

A farm manager decides to tear down an existing silo, dig out the concrete pad and replace it with a new one, and build a new silo on the same spot. All of the following costs will be associated with the new silo:

Demolish existing silo	$8,000
Dig out old concrete pad	4,000
Pour new concrete pad	12,000
Construct new silo	90,000
Total	$114,000

Lump-Sum Purchases

A farmer might buy an entire farm as part of a single purchase price. This purchase may include land, buildings, machinery, and so forth. If so, the proper accounting is to apportion the purchase price to the individual assets based on their individual market values. It is possible that the sum of the individual asset market values will differ from the purchase price. If so, allocate the purchase price based on each asset's proportion of the total market value of the assets.

EXAMPLE

Mr. Jones buys Hillside Farm for $550,000. The property is comprised of 100 acres of land, a farmhouse, barn, silo, and tractor. An appraiser provides individual market values for each of the assets. The total of these market values is $50,000 more than the amount paid for the property. In the following table, the price paid is allocated to the individual assets.

Asset Description	Market Value	Proportion of Total	Price Allocation
Land	80,000	13.3%	$73,150
Farmhouse	250,000	41.7%	229,350
Barn	150,000	25.0%	137,500
Silo	100,000	16.7%	91,850
Tractor	20,000	3.3%	18,150
	$600,000	100.0%	$550,000

These allocated amounts are then recognized as fixed assets with the following journal entry:

	Debit	Credit
Land [asset account]	73,150	
Buildings [asset account]	458,700	
Tractors [asset account]	18,150	
Cash [asset account]		550,000

The Purpose of Depreciation

The purpose of depreciation is to charge to expense a portion of an asset that relates to the revenue generated by that asset. This is called the matching principle, where revenues and expenses both appear in the income statement in the same reporting period, which gives the best view of how well a farm has performed in a given accounting period. The trouble with this matching concept is that there is usually only a tenuous connection between the generation of revenue and a specific asset.

To get around this linkage problem, we usually assume a steady rate of depreciation over the useful life of each asset, so that we approximate a linkage between the recognition of revenues and expenses. This approximation threatens our credulity even more when a farm uses accelerated depreciation, since the main reason for using it is to defer taxes (and not to better match revenues and expenses).

If we were not to use depreciation at all, we would be forced to charge all assets to expense as soon as we buy them. This would result in large losses in the months when the purchase transaction occurs, followed by unusually high profitability in those periods when the corresponding amount of revenue is recognized, with no offsetting expense. Thus, a farm that does not use depreciation will have front-loaded expenses, and extremely variable financial results.

> **Note:** When an intangible asset (such as a patent) is depreciated, it is referred to as *amortization*. Depreciation applies to tangible assets.

Depreciation Concepts

There are three factors to consider in the calculation of depreciation, which are as follows:

- *Useful life*. This is the time period over which it is expected that an asset will be productive. Past an asset's useful life, it is no longer cost-effective to continue operating the asset, so the farm would dispose of it or stop using it. Depreciation is recognized over the useful life of an asset.
- *Salvage value*. When a farm eventually disposes of an asset, it may be able to sell the asset for some reduced amount, which is the salvage value. Depreciation is calculated based on the asset cost, less any estimated salvage value. If salvage value is expected to be quite small, it is generally ignored for the purpose of calculating depreciation.

EXAMPLE

Sunlight Farm buys a tractor for $75,000 and estimates that its salvage value will be $15,000 in five years, when it plans to dispose of the asset. This means that Sunlight will depreciate $60,000 of the asset cost over five years, leaving $15,000 of the cost remaining at the end of that time. Sunlight expects to then sell the asset for $15,000, which will eliminate it from Sunlight's accounting records.

- *Depreciation method*. Depreciation expense can be calculated using an accelerated depreciation method, or evenly over the useful life of the asset. The advantage of using an accelerated method is that a farm can recognize more depreciation early in the life of a fixed asset, which defers some income tax expense recognition to a later period. The advantage of using a steady depreciation rate is the ease of calculation. Examples of accelerated depreciation methods are the double declining balance and sum-of-the-years' digits methods. The primary method for steady depreciation is the straight-line method.

The *mid-month convention* states that, no matter when a fixed asset is purchased in a month, it is assumed to have been purchased in the middle of the month for depreciation purposes. Thus, if a fixed asset was purchased on January 5th, assume that it was bought on January 15th; or, if it was acquired on January 28, still assume that it was bought on January 15th. By doing so, it is easier to calculate a standard half-month of depreciation for the first month of ownership.

If the farm accountant chooses to use the mid-month convention, this also means that he should record a half-month of depreciation for the *last* month of the asset's useful life. By doing so, the two half-month depreciation calculations equal one full month of depreciation.

Many farm accountants prefer to use full-month depreciation in the first month of ownership, irrespective of the actual date of purchase within the month, so that they can slightly accelerate their recognition of depreciation, which in turn reduces their taxable income in the near term.

Accelerated Depreciation

Accelerated depreciation is the depreciation of fixed assets at a very fast rate early in their useful lives. The primary reason for using accelerated depreciation is to reduce the reported amount of taxable income over the first few years of an asset's life, so that a farm pays a smaller amount of income taxes during those early years. Later on, when most of the depreciation will have already been recognized, the effect reverses, so there will be less depreciation available to shelter taxable income. The result is that a farm pays more income taxes in later years. Thus, the net effect of accelerated depreciation is the deferral of income taxes to later time periods.

A secondary reason for using accelerated depreciation is that it may actually reflect the usage pattern of the underlying assets, if they experience heavy usage early in their useful lives.

There are several calculations available for accelerated depreciation, such as the double declining balance method and the sum of the years' digits method. We will describe these methods in the following sub-sections.

All of the depreciation methods end up recognizing the same amount of depreciation, which is the cost of the fixed asset less any expected salvage value. The only difference between the various methods is the speed with which depreciation is recognized.

Accelerated depreciation requires additional depreciation calculations and record keeping, so some farm accountants avoid it for that reason (though fixed asset software can readily overcome this issue). They may also ignore accelerated depreciation if they are not consistently earning taxable income, which takes away the primary reason for using it. Farmer accountants may also ignore accelerated depreciation if they have a relatively small amount of fixed assets, so that the tax effect of using accelerated depreciation is minimal.

Sum-of-the-Years' Digits Method

The sum of the years' digits (SYD) method is used to calculate depreciation on an accelerated basis. Use the following formula to calculate it:

$$\text{Depreciation percentage} = \frac{\text{Number of estimated years of life as of beginning of the year}}{\text{Sum of the years' digits}}$$

The following table contains examples of the sum of the years' digits noted in the denominator of the preceding formula.

Sample Sum of the Years' Digits Calculation

Total Depreciation Period	Initial Sum of the Years' Digits	Calculation
2 years	3	1 + 2
3 years	6	1 + 2 + 3
4 years	10	1 + 2 + 3 + 4
5 years	15	1 + 2 + 3 + 4 + 5

The concept is illustrated in the following example.

EXAMPLE

The manager of Bonnie View Farm buys a manure spreader for $10,000. The equipment has no estimated salvage value and a useful life of five years. The farm accountant calculates the annual sum of the years' digits depreciation for this machine as:

Year	Number of estimated years of life as of beginning of the year	SYD Calculation	Depreciation Percentage	Annual Depreciation
1	5	5/15	33.33%	$3,333
2	4	4/15	26.67%	2,667
3	3	3/15	20.00%	2,000
4	2	2/15	13.33%	1,333
5	1	1/15	6.67%	667
Totals	15		100.00%	$10,000

Double-Declining Balance Method

The double declining balance (DDB) method is a form of accelerated depreciation. To calculate the double-declining balance depreciation rate, divide the number of years of useful life of an asset into 100 percent, and multiply the result by two. The formula is:

$$(100\% \div \text{Years of useful life}) \times 2$$

The DDB calculation proceeds until the asset's salvage value is reached, after which depreciation ends.

EXAMPLE

The manager of Brookside Farm purchases a potato planter for $50,000. It has an estimated salvage value of $5,000 and a useful life of five years. The calculation of the double declining balance depreciation rate is:

$$(100\% \div \text{Years of useful life}) \times 2 = 40\%$$

By applying the 40% rate, the farm accountant arrives at the following table of depreciation charges per year:

Year	Book Value at Beginning of Year	Depreciation Percentage	DDB Depreciation	Book Value Net of Depreciation
1	$50,000	40%	$20,000	$30,000
2	30,000	40%	12,000	18,000
3	18,000	40%	7,200	10,800
4	10,800	40%	4,320	6,480
5	6,480	40%	1,480	5,000
Total			$45,000	

Note that the depreciation in the fifth and final year is only for $1,480, rather than the $3,240 that would be indicated by the 40% depreciation rate. The reason for the smaller depreciation charge is that Brookside stops any further depreciation once the remaining book value declines to the amount of the estimated salvage value.

A variation on the double-declining balance method is the 150% declining balance method, which recognizes depreciation at a somewhat less aggressive rate.

Straight-Line Method

If a farm accountant elects not to use accelerated depreciation, he can instead use the straight-line method, where it depreciates an asset at the same standard rate throughout its useful life. Under the straight-line method of depreciation, recognize depreciation expense evenly over the estimated useful life of an asset. The straight-line calculation steps are:

1. Subtract the estimated salvage value of the asset from the amount at which it is recorded on the books.
2. Determine the estimated useful life of the asset. It is easiest to use a standard useful life for each class of assets.
3. Divide the estimated useful life (in years) into 1 to arrive at the straight-line depreciation rate.
4. Multiply the depreciation rate by the asset cost (less salvage value).

EXAMPLE

Murray Family Farms purchases a broadcast seeder for $6,000. It has an estimated salvage value of $1,000 and a useful life of five years. The farm accountant calculates the annual straight-line depreciation for the seeder as:

1. Purchase cost of $6,000 – Estimated salvage value of $1,000 = Depreciable asset cost of $5,000
2. 1 ÷ 5-Year useful life = 20% Depreciation rate per year
3. 20% Depreciation rate × $5,000 Depreciable asset cost = $1,000 Annual depreciation

---

Units of Activity Method

Under the units of activity method, the amount of depreciation charged to expense varies in direct proportion to the amount of asset usage. Thus, more depreciation is charged in periods when there is more asset usage and less depreciation in periods when there is less asset usage. It is the most accurate method for charging depreciation, since it links closely to the wear and tear on assets. However, it also requires the tracking of asset usage, which means that its use is generally limited to more expensive assets. Also, it is necessary to estimate total usage over the life of the asset.

> **Tip:** Do not use the units of activity method if there is not a significant difference in asset usage from period to period. Otherwise, the farm accountant will spend a great deal of time tracking asset usage and will be rewarded with a depreciation expense that varies little from the results that would have been experienced with the straight-line method (which is far easier to calculate).

Follow these steps to calculate depreciation under the units of activity method:

1. Estimate the total number of hours of usage of the asset, or the total amount of activity to be produced by it over its useful life.
2. Subtract any estimated salvage value from the capitalized cost of the asset, and divide the total estimated usage from this net depreciable cost. This yields the depreciation cost per hour of usage or other unit of activity.

3. Multiply the number of hours of usage or units of actual activity by the depreciation cost per hour or unit of activity, which results in the total depreciation expense for the accounting period.

If the estimated number of hours of usage or units of activity changes over time, incorporate these changes into the calculation of the depreciation cost per hour or unit of activity. This will alter the depreciation expense on a go-forward basis.

EXAMPLE

The manager of Idlewild Farm has just purchased a cotton picker that he only expects to use during cotton picking season. The cost of the picker is $90,000. The manager expects to use the picker for 5,000 hours and then sell it off at a salvage value of $40,000, which leaves $50,000 to be depreciated. Since picker usage depends on the time of year, the manager elects to use the units of activity method for depreciation. Accordingly, the depreciation rate is set at $10 per hour of usage (calculated as $50,000 to be depreciated ÷ 5,000 hours). During the first month of operation, Idlewild runs the picker for 420 hours, and so charges $4,200 to depreciation expense.

MACRS Depreciation

MACRS depreciation is the tax depreciation system used in the United States. MACRS is an acronym for Modified Accelerated Cost Recovery System. Under MACRS, fixed assets are assigned to a specific asset class. The Internal Revenue Service has published a complete set of depreciation tables for each of these classes. The classes are noted in the following table. Those assets specifically pertaining to farm equipment have been stated in bold.

MACRS Table

Class	Depreciation Period	Description
3-year property	3 years	**Tractor units for over-the-road use**, race horses over 2 years old when placed in service, any other horse over 12 years old when placed in service, qualified rent-to-own property
5-year property	5 years	Automobiles, taxis, buses, trucks, computers and peripheral equipment, office equipment, any property used in research and experimentation, **breeding cattle and dairy cattle**, appliances and etc. used in residential rental real estate activity, certain green energy property
7-year property	7 years	Office furniture and fixtures, **agricultural machinery and equipment**, any property not designated as being in another class, natural gas gathering lines
10-year property	10 years	Vessels, barges, tugs, **single-purpose agricultural or horticultural structures, trees/vines bearing fruits or nuts**, qualified small electric meter and smart electric grid systems
15-year property	15 years	Certain land improvements (such as shrubbery, fences, roads, sidewalks and bridges), retail motor fuel outlets, municipal wastewater treatment plants, clearing and grading land improvements for gas utility property, electric transmission property, natural gas distribution lines
20-year property	20 years	**Farm buildings** (other than those noted under 10-year property), municipal sewers not categorized as 25-year property, the initial clearing and grading of land for electric utility transmission and distribution plants
25-year property	25 years	Property that is an integral part of the water distribution facilities, municipal sewers
Residential rental property	27.5 years	Any building or structure where 80% or more of its gross rental income is from dwelling units
Nonresidential real property	39 years	An office building, store, or warehouse that is not residential property or has a class life of less than 27.5 years

The depreciation rates associated with the more common asset classes are noted in the following table.

Depreciation Rates for MACRS Asset Classes

Recovery Year	3-Year Property	5-Year Property	7-Year Property	10-Year Property	15-Year Property	20-Year Property
1	33.33%	20.00%	14.29%	10.00%	5.00%	3.750%
2	44.45%	32.00%	24.49%	18.00%	9.50%	7.219%
3	14.81%	19.20%	17.49%	14.40%	8.55%	6.677%
4	7.41%	11.52%	12.49%	11.52%	7.70%	6.177%
5		11.52%	8.93%	9.22%	6.93%	5.713%
6		5.76%	8.92%	7.37%	6.23%	5.285%
7			8.93%	6.55%	5.90%	4.888%
8			4.46%	6.55%	5.90%	4.522%
9				6.56%	5.91%	4.462%
10				6.55%	5.90%	4.461%
11				3.28%	5.91%	4.462%
12					5.90%	4.461%
13					5.91%	4.462%
14					5.90%	4.461%
15					5.91%	4.462%
16					2.95%	4.461%
17						4.462%
18						4.461%
19						4.462%
20						4.461%
21						2.231%

Depreciation is calculated for tax reporting purposes by aggregating assets into the various classes noted in the preceding table and using the depreciation rates for each class. MACRS ignores salvage value.

The MACRS depreciation rates are used to determine the depreciation expense for taxable income, while the other methods described earlier are used to arrive at the depreciation expense for net income. Since these depreciation methods have differing results, there will be a temporary difference between the book values of fixed assets under the two methods, which will gradually be resolved over their useful lives. Report the difference between depreciation used for calculating taxable income and for the financial statements as a reconciling item in a farm's federal income tax return.

The Depreciation of Land

Nearly all fixed assets have a useful life, after which they no longer contribute to the operations of a farm or they stop generating revenue. During this useful life, they are depreciated, which reduces their cost to what they are supposed to be worth at the end of their useful lives. Land, however, has no definitive useful life, so there is no way to depreciate it.

The Depreciation of Land Improvements

Land improvements are enhancements to a plot of land to make it more usable. If these improvements have a useful life, depreciate them. If there is no way to estimate a useful life, do not depreciate the cost of the improvements.

If land is being prepared for its intended purpose, include these costs in the cost of the land asset. They are not depreciated. Examples of such costs are:

- Demolishing an existing building
- Clearing and leveling the land

If functionality is being added to the land and the expenditures have a useful life, record them in a separate Land Improvements account. Examples of land improvements are:

- Drainage and irrigation systems
- Fencing
- Landscaping
- Parking lots and walkways

A special item is the ongoing cost of landscaping. This is a period cost, not a fixed asset, and so should be charged to expense as incurred.

EXAMPLE

The manager of Durham Ranch buys a parcel of land for $1,000,000. Since it is a purchase of land, the ranch accountant cannot depreciate the cost. Durham then razes a building that was located on the property at a cost of $25,000, fills in the old foundation for $5,000, and levels the land for $50,000. All of these costs are to prepare the land for its intended purpose, so they are all added to the cost of the land. Durham cannot depreciate these costs.

The ranch manager intends to use the land as a mountain biking trail area, so he spends $40,000 to create a parking lot and cut trails. The ranch accountant estimates that these improvements have a useful life of 10 years. These costs should be recorded in the Land Improvements account and depreciated over 10 years.

Depreciation Accounting Entries

The basic depreciation entry is to debit the depreciation expense account (which appears in the income statement) and credit the accumulated depreciation account (which appears in the balance sheet as a contra account that reduces the amount of fixed assets). Over time, the accumulated depreciation balance will continue to increase as more depreciation is added to it, until such time as it equals the original cost of the asset. At that time, stop recording any depreciation expense, since the cost of the asset has now been reduced to zero.

The journal entry for depreciation can be a simple two-line entry designed to accommodate all types of fixed assets, or it may be subdivided into separate entries for each type of fixed asset.

EXAMPLE

The farm accountant for Hillcrest Farm calculates that it should have $25,000 of depreciation expense in the current month. The entry is:

	Debit	Credit
Depreciation expense [expense account]	25,000	
Accumulated depreciation [contra asset account]		25,000

In the following month, Hillcrest's accountant decides to show a higher level of precision at the expense account level and instead elects to apportion the $25,000 of depreciation among different expense accounts, so that each class of asset has a separate depreciation charge. The entry is:

	Debit	Credit
Depreciation expense – Breeding livestock [expense account]	4,000	
Depreciation expense – Buildings [expense account]	8,000	
Depreciation expense – Perennial crops [expense account]	6,000	
Depreciation expense – Tractors [expense account]	5,000	
Depreciation expense – Vehicles [expense account]	2,000	
Accumulated depreciation [contra asset account]		25,000

Accumulated Depreciation

When an asset is sold or otherwise disposed of, all related accumulated depreciation is removed from the accounting records at the same time. Otherwise, an unusually large amount of accumulated depreciation will build up on the balance sheet.

EXAMPLE

Oak Hill Farm has $1,000,000 of fixed assets, against which it has charged $380,000 of accumulated depreciation. This results in the following presentation on the farm's balance sheet:

Fixed assets	$1,000,000
Less: Accumulated depreciation	(380,000)
Net fixed assets	$620,000

The farm manager then sells equipment for $80,000 that had an original cost of $140,000, and for which accumulated depreciation of $50,000 had already been recorded. The farm accountant records the sale with this journal entry:

	Debit	Credit
Cash [asset account]	80,000	
Accumulated depreciation [contra asset account]	50,000	
Loss on asset sale [gain/loss account]	10,000	
Fixed assets [asset account]		140,000

As a result of this entry, Oak Hill's balance sheet presentation of fixed assets has changed, so that fixed assets before accumulated depreciation have declined to $860,000 and accumulated depreciation has declined to $330,000. The new presentation is:

Fixed assets	$860,000
Less: Accumulated depreciation	(330,000)
Net fixed assets	$530,000

The amount of net fixed assets declined by $90,000 as a result of the asset sale, which is the sum of the $80,000 cash proceeds and the $10,000 loss resulting from the asset sale.

Asset Disposal Accounting

There are two scenarios under which a farm may dispose of a fixed asset. The first situation arises when a fixed asset is being eliminated without receiving any payment in return. This is a common situation when a fixed asset is being scrapped because it is obsolete or no longer in use, and there is no resale market for it. In this case, reverse any accumulated depreciation and reverse the original asset cost. If the asset is fully depreciated, that is the extent of the entry.

EXAMPLE

The manager of Cloverdale Farm buys a grain cart for $10,000 and recognizes $1,000 of depreciation per year over the following ten years. At that time, the cart is not only fully depreciated, but also ready for the scrap heap. The farm manager gives away the cart for free and records the following entry.

	Debit	Credit
Accumulated depreciation [contra asset account]	10,000	
Equipment asset [asset account]		10,000

What if the farm manager was unable to give away the cart, and instead had to pay a junk dealer $100 to take it? In this case, the $100 is added to the entry as a cash reduction and there is now a $100 loss. The entry would be:

	Debit	Credit
Accumulated depreciation [contra asset account]	10,000	
Loss on asset disposal [gain/loss account]	100	
Equipment asset [asset account]		10,000
Cash [asset account]		100

A variation on this situation is to write off a fixed asset that has not yet been completely depreciated. In this case, write off the remaining undepreciated amount of the asset to a loss account.

EXAMPLE

To use the same example, the farm manager gives away the grain cart after eight years, when the farm has not yet depreciated $2,000 of the asset's original $10,000 cost. In this case, the farm accountant records the following entry:

	Debit	Credit
Loss on asset disposal [gain/loss account]	2,000	
Accumulated depreciation [contra asset account]	8,000	
Equipment asset [asset account]		10,000

The second scenario arises when an asset is sold, so that the farm receives cash in exchange for the fixed asset being sold. Depending upon the price paid and the remaining amount of depreciation that has not yet been charged to expense, this can result in either a gain or a loss on sale of the asset.

EXAMPLE

Cloverdale's farm manager still disposes of the $10,000 grain cart, but does so after seven years, and sells it for $3,500 in cash. In this case, the farm accountant has already recorded $7,000 of depreciation expense. The disposal entry is:

	Debit	Credit
Cash [asset account]	3,500	
Accumulated depreciation [contra asset account]	7,000	
Gain on asset disposal [gain/loss account]		500
Equipment asset [asset account]		10,000

What if the manager had sold the machine for $2,500 instead of $3,500? Then there would be a loss of $500 on the sale. The entry would be:

	Debit	Credit
Cash [asset account]	2,500	
Accumulated depreciation [contra asset account]	7,000	
Loss on asset disposal [gain/loss account]	500	
Equipment asset [asset account]		10,000

The "loss on asset disposal" or "gain on asset disposal" accounts noted in the preceding sample entries are called disposal accounts. They may be combined into a single account or used separately to store gains and losses resulting from the disposal of fixed assets.

Impairment Write-downs

A fixed asset is considered to be impaired when its carrying amount is not recoverable and exceeds its fair value. The carrying amount is not recoverable when it exceeds the sum of the cash flows expected to result from the use of the asset over its remaining useful life and final disposition. The amount of an impairment loss is the difference between an asset's carrying amount and its fair value. Once this loss is recognized, it reduces the carrying amount of the asset, possibly by a substantial amount.

Impairments are unlikely to apply to most farm operations for the following reasons:

- Only the most expensive assets are generally subjected to an impairment review, so most farm assets will never be examined.
- Farm assets are being depreciated, so their carrying amounts may be quite low, leaving little room for an impairment charge.

Asset impairment is a complex topic that goes well beyond our one-paragraph description. If an asset appears to be at risk of impairment, consult with a certified public accountant for advice on how to proceed.

Summary

From the perspective of the accountant, the tracking of fixed assets can be quite time-consuming. Consequently, we recommend setting a high capitalization limit in order to charge most purchases to expense at once, rather than recording them as fixed assets.

Depreciation is one of the central concerns of the farm accountant, since the broad range of available methods can result in significant differences in the amount of depreciation expense recorded in each period. Generally, adopt the straight-line depreciation method to minimize the amount of depreciation calculations, unless the usage rate of the assets involved more closely matches a different depreciation method. Farmers concerned with reducing their tax liabilities will be more likely to use the MACRS depreciation rates when calculating their taxable income.

Chapter 9
Non-Current Farm Assets

Introduction

Non-current assets are assets that will be retained for more than one year. Given the expected length of usage, these assets are not recorded as inventory, but rather within a different class of long-term assets. Unless animals have such short productive lives that they are classified as inventory, they should be classified as non-current assets. This includes breeding animals, livestock, and production animals.

We previously covered the treatment of costs related to raising crops for harvest. The situation is different for the development costs of land, trees and vines, intermediate-life plants, and animals. These development costs are discussed in the following sub-sections.

Land Development Costs

Land development costs are incurred in order to bring land into a suitable condition for agricultural use, as well as to maintain its productive condition. Examples of permanent land developments are clearing, initial leveling, and terracing. These developments all involve alterations to the grade and contour of the land. A land development asset should have an indefinite life if properly maintained. There are also limited-life developments, which may include ditches, fencing, levees, ponds, and wells.

Permanent land development costs should be capitalized. These costs are not depreciated, since the asset is considered to have an indefinite useful life. Limited-life development costs should be depreciated over the estimated useful life of the land development.

Trees and Vines

It can take a number of years before orchards, vineyards and groves mature enough to begin commercial production, which may then continue for a number of years. During the development period, it may be necessary to engage in grafting, pruning, spraying, cultivation, and other activities.

Cultural costs during the development period should be accumulated. These costs include stakes and wires, grafting, and the labor associated with pruning and forming. If any products are sold before commercial production begins, the net proceeds should be applied to the capitalized cost of the trees or vines.

All limited-life land development costs associated with orchards, vineyards, and groves should be capitalized during the development period.

Once production begins in commercial quantities, the accumulated costs are depreciated over the estimated useful life of the orchard, vineyard, or grove. During this time, the accumulated costs are reported on the balance sheet as a non-current asset.

EXAMPLE

Blossom Orchards invests $80,000 in the development of a cherry orchard. This involves the accumulation of many costs over six years; in aggregate, the entry that records this expenditure is:

	Debit	Credit
Perennial Crops [asset account]	80,000	
Cash [asset account]		80,000

The orchard is expected to be in production for the next 20 years, so the $80,000 development cost is depreciated over that period. The annual depreciation entry for the orchard is:

	Debit	Credit
Depreciation expense [expense account]	4,000	
Accumulated depreciation [contra asset account]		4,000

Any costs incurred once the commercial product phase is reached are to be charged to expense as incurred.

In essence, the accounting for trees and vines matches what would be used for a constructed asset. Costs are accumulated during the "construction" phase, and charged to expense through depreciation once the asset has been put into service.

Intermediate-Life Plants

Intermediate-life plants are plants that have a growth and production cycle exceeding one year, but less than those of trees and vines. Examples are artichokes, asparagus, and grazing grasses. During their development, a farmer may engage in land preparation, plant purchases, and cultural care. Development costs should be accumulated until production begins in commercial quantities. At that point, depreciate the costs over the estimated useful life of the plantings. The useful life chosen for depreciation may vary, depending on regional differences and other factors.

The cost of intermediate-life plants are reported on the balance sheet as a non-current asset. A farm should disclose in the footnotes attached to the financial statements the accumulated costs for intermediate-life plants, as well as their estimated useful lives.

Valuation of Raised Breeding Livestock

Raised breeding livestock are considered non-current assets, since the expectation is that they will be retained for a protracted period of time. This type of livestock should be valued at the full cost of raising the animals in order to be in compliance with GAAP. In short, all costs of developing animals, both direct and indirect, are to be accumulated until the animals reach their maturity and are then reclassified to a productive function. Consequently, the following costs must be tracked for raised breeding livestock:

- Breeding fees
- Cost of raised feed
- Cost of purchased feed
- Farm labor

- Fuel
- Supplies
- Veterinarian services
- Other related costs

The most GAAP-compliant way to track these costs is to use the full absorption method. This is a comprehensive cost tracking methodology under which the farm accountant compiles all costs incurred that relate to the raised breeding livestock. These costs are stored in the Breeding Livestock non-current asset account. The capitalized cost of the animals is then depreciated over their useful lives. Depreciation begins when the animals reach maturity and are reclassified as production animals. The amount depreciated is the costs that have been accumulated up until that point. Depreciation is based on the following:

- Accumulated costs
- Less any estimated salvage value
- Spread over the estimated productive lives of the animals

Thus, the depreciation used for raised breeding livestock matches what is used for other fixed assets.

When an animal is eventually sold, the farm accountant compares the price received to the book value of the animal, and recognizes a gain or loss on the sale, as would be the case for any other fixed asset disposition. The calculation of gains and losses is covered in the Fixed Assets and Depreciation chapter.

If an animal dies, the same accounting applies as though the animal had been sold at a price of zero. In this situation, the book value of the animal is written off and the farm recognizes a loss for the entire net book value of the animal.

Special Poultry Considerations

The production cost of a chicken that is being raised for egg-laying purposes shall include its initial cost, plus materials and labor, and a reasonable amount of allocated indirect costs during the prematurity period. These costs are then amortized over the egg-laying period, less any estimated salvage value for the chickens.

Animal Cost Tracking

The most detailed level of cost tracking under the GAAP requirements for raised breeding livestock prior to their maturity is to maintain valuation records for each animal. This can work when each animal has been individually identified, such as with a numeric tag. However, nearly all costs incurred are for an entire herd or flock, not for an individual animal. Consequently, the farm accountant will find it easier to accumulate all costs for the herd or flock as a group, and then allocate the costs to each individual animal in the herd or flock.

Base Value Method

The accumulation of costs at the level of detail required by GAAP is time-consuming for the farm accountant. An alternative approach suggested by the Farm Financial Standards Council is to designate a cost for each animal using the *base value method*. Under this approach (which is not supported anywhere in GAAP), a cost is assigned to raised breeding livestock that is based on a base value from a reputable source. This value is assigned when an animal enters the breeding herd or flock; the value appears in the Breeding Livestock account, which is a non-current asset account. Every time a raised breeding animal moves into a new age category, it is assigned the base value for animals in that category. Whenever an animal shifts into a new age category, this is called a *transfer point*.

The key accounting events under the base value method are as follows:

- *Growth*. During the growing years of an animal, all related costs are charged to expense as incurred. This greatly reduces the cost tracking work of the farm accountant.
- *Entry into herd*. Once the animal enters the breeding herd, it is assigned a base value.
- *Transfer points*. Every time an animal shifts into a new age group, its base value is altered in the accounting records. To simplify the situation, the accountant can use just a single transfer point, for example, when females are bred and when males enter breeding service.
- *Sale*. When an animal is sold, the farm accountant recognizes a gain or loss on the sale by comparing the sale price to the most recent base value of the animal.

Under the base value method, changes in the base value of an animal are recorded as changes in the non-current asset, as well as changes in farm income. Base value is not depreciated.

If a farm accountant elects to use the base value method, he should cite the following information in the disclosures that accompany the farm's financial statements:

- The source of the base values used
- The animal age groupings associated with each base value (such as yearlings and 2-year-olds)

There are several important differences between GAAP requirements and the base value method. First, the GAAP approach capitalizes all costs incurred during the development stage of an animal, while the base value method requires these costs to be charged to expense as incurred. Second, the base value method works with estimates of the value of mature animals, rather than their actual cost. Even if the farm accountant maintains detailed documentation supporting his positions for the use of certain base values, these amounts are not the same as actual costs, and could be significantly different from those costs.

Non-Current Investments

We now shift to a discussion of the investment that a farm may have in a cooperative, since this is considered a non-current farm asset. All other accounting related to cooperatives is located in the Cooperative Accounting chapter.

Member patrons provide a large part or all of the capital needed by cooperatives in order to function. This capital may be in the form of:

- Cash paid in when the cooperative is founded
- Profits retained by the cooperative thereafter, rather than being distributed to the patrons
- Noncash patronage allocations, rather than paying cash back to the patrons

When a farm has invested in a cooperative, this amount is classified as a non-current asset, under the assumption that the investment will not be converted back into cash within the next year.

EXAMPLE

A farm manager buys a membership in a local cooperative for $25,000, as shown in the following entry:

	Debit	Credit
Investments [asset account]	25,000	
Cash [asset account]		25,000

The cooperative generates $2,000 of income to which the farm is entitled, but retains the cash rather than distributing it. The entry by the farm accountant is:

	Debit	Credit
Investments [asset account]	2,000	
Miscellaneous income [asset account]		2,000

The voting rights in a cooperative are usually based on either each member receiving one vote or a limited weighting, rather than the actual proportion of equity ownership held. These investments are not considered to be equity securities, and so are not read-ily marketable or transferable. Usually, an investment in a cooperative can only be transferred back to the cooperative. Given these restrictions, an investment in a coop-erative is similar to an investment in a partnership or joint venture.

A patron should record the cost of an investment in a cooperative at its cost. Cost is considered to be the amount of any cash investment, plus the amount stated on all written notices of allocation issued to the patron by the cooperative that are in the form of:

- Capital equity credits
- Certificates of equity
- Per-unit retains
- Revolving fund certificates

Patronage refund payments received by a member patron from a cooperative are treated by the member as a reduction in its investment account.

EXAMPLE

A farm currently has an investment balance of $32,000 in a local cooperative. The cooperative pays out a patronage refund of $1,800. Once the funds are received, this reduces the farm's investment balance to $30,200, as triggered by the following journal entry:

	Debit	Credit
Cash [asset account]	1,800	
Investments [asset account]		1,800

If a patron cannot recover the full carrying amount of an investment in a cooperative, the amount of the recognized investment should be reduced. This may be the case when a cooperative has experienced unallocated losses that exceed its unallocated eq-uities. In such a case, the patron should recognize a loss on the investment for the patron's share of the difference between the unallocated losses and unallocated equi-ties. An alternative method may be used, if appropriate. The only case in which a loss is not recognized is when the patron can demonstrate that the carrying amount of the investment can be recovered, and that this event is probable.

When deciding whether the carrying amount of an investment should be reduced, the following factors should be considered:

- Whether the unallocated losses were caused by nonrecurring, isolated, and identifiable events
- Whether the cooperative has a long history of profitability and only experi-ences infrequent losses that have been offset by unallocated earnings or equi-ties

- Whether the investor has ceased patronizing the cooperative or expects to do so, and for an extended period of time

Retains are the amounts withheld by cooperatives from distribution to patrons. Instead, these amounts are allocated to the capital accounts of the patrons. If there is no expectation that retains will be redeemed in the current year by the patron, the patron should classify them as noncurrent assets.

Summary

We presented the valuation issues related to a number of farm-specific non-current assets in this chapter. For a detailed examination of how the costs associated with these assets are gradually charged to expense, see the Fixed Assets and Depreciation chapter.

When tracking the investment in a cooperative, the key issue to be aware of is whether the cooperative has the ability to pay back the investment. If not, the farm accountant will need to immediately recognize a loss on the investment, which could represent a substantial loss for a farm.

Chapter 10
Payables Accounting

Introduction

Accounts payable refers to the aggregate amount of a farm's short-term obligations to pay suppliers for products and services that the farm purchased on credit. In this chapter, we cover the essentials of accounts payable under the assumption that an accounting software package is in use. This means that a vendor master file is in use, that the accountant has a standard system for assigning names to suppliers, and uses an adequate filing system. All of these topics are covered in the following pages, along with discussions of Form 1099 reporting and the accounting entries that are automatically produced by a payables software module.

> **Related Podcast Episodes:** Episodes 13, 22, 81, 82, and 138 of the Accounting Best Practices Podcast discuss payables. They are available at: **accountingtools.com/podcasts** or **iTunes**

Accounting for Accounts Payable

Accounts payable refers to the collective obligation to pay suppliers for goods and services that were acquired on credit. The day-to-day accounting for accounts payable is relatively simple. Whenever the farm receives an invoice from a supplier, the farm accountant enters the vendor number of the supplier into the accounting software, which automatically assigns a default general ledger account number from the vendor master file to the invoice. The vendor master file contains essential information about each supplier, including a default account number to which it is assumed that most invoices from that supplier will be charged.

EXAMPLE

Milagro Farm receives an invoice from Mary Aleppo, which provides the farm with veterinary services. In the vendor master file, the accountant has already assigned general ledger account number 5050, Veterinarian and Medical Expense, to Ms. Aleppo. Thus, when the accountant enters the invoice into the accounts payable module of the accounting software, the system automatically assigns the invoice to account 5050.

If the invoice is for goods or services other than the predetermined general ledger account number, the accountant can manually enter a different account number, which is only good for that specific invoice – it does not become the new default account for the supplier. In short, the pre-assignment of account numbers to suppliers greatly simplifies the accounting for payables.

> **Tip:** At the end of each accounting period, print a report that shows the amount of expense charged to each account in each of the past 12 months. Compare the expense balance in the most current period to prior periods; if there is a significant difference, it may be caused by the incorrect assignment of a supplier invoice to an account. If so, investigate the account and see if a different default account should be assigned to the supplier whose invoice caused the discrepancy.

The accounting software should automatically create a credit to the accounts payable account whenever the accountant records a supplier invoice. Thus, a typical entry might be:

	Debit	Credit
Supplies expense [expense account]	xxx	
Accounts payable [liability account]		xxx

Later, when the farm pays suppliers (typically during a weekly check run), the accounting system eliminates the accounts payable balance with the following entry:

	Debit	Credit
Accounts payable [liability account]	xxx	
Cash [asset account]		xxx

It is possible that small debit or credit residual balances may appear in the accounts payable account. These balances may be caused by any number of issues, such as credit memos issued by suppliers which the farm accountant does not plan to use, or amounts that the farm had valid cause not to pay. Occasionally run the aged accounts payable report to spot these items. Do not use journal entries to clear them out, since this will not be recognized by the report writing software that generates the aged accounts payable report. Instead, always create debit or credit memo transactions that are recognized by the report writer; this will flush the residual balances from the aged accounts payable report.

There is usually an option in the accounting software that automatically generates the necessary debit memo or credit memo. As an example, a farm may have been granted a credit memo by a supplier for $100, to be used to reduce the amount of an outstanding account payable. The accountant enters the credit memo screen in the accounting software, enters the name of the supplier and the credit memo amount, and selects the expense account that will be offset.

The journal entry that the software automatically generates could be as follows:

	Debit	Credit
Accounts payable [liability account]	100	
Supplies expense [expense account]		100

If a supplier offers a discount in exchange for the early payment of an invoice, the farm is not paying the full amount of the invoice. Instead, that portion of the invoice related to the discount is charged to a separate account. If an accounting software package is used, the system automatically allocates the appropriate amount to this separate account. For example, an entry to take a 2% early payment discount on a supplier invoice might be:

	Debit	Credit
Accounts payable [liability account]	100	
Cash [asset account]		98
Discounts taken [contra expense account]		2

This entry flushes out the full amount of the original account payable, so that no residual balance remains in the accounting records to be paid.

At month-end, it may be necessary to accrue for expenses when goods or services have been received by the farm, but for which no supplier invoice has yet been received. To do so, examine the receiving log just after month-end to see which receipts do not have an associated invoice. Also, consider reviewing the expense accruals for the preceding month; a supplier that issues invoices late will probably do so on a repetitive basis, so the last set of expense accruals typically provides clues to what should be included in the next set of accruals.

When a month-end expense accrual is created, it is done with a reversing journal entry, so that the accounting system automatically reverses the expense at the beginning of the following month. Otherwise, the accountant will be at risk of forgetting that an expense was accrued, and may leave it on the books for a number of months. Also, charge the accrued expense to a liability account separate from the accounts payable account, so that all accruals are separately tracked. A common liability account for this is "accrued accounts payable." Thus, a typical accrued expense entry might be:

	Debit	Credit
Rent expense (expense)	xxx	
Accrued accounts payable (liability)		xxx

If a period-end accrual is made for income taxes, the tax could be recorded within the accrued accounts payable account. Alternatively, it could be recorded separately, especially if the amount is so large that management wants to report it separately in the balance sheet. An example of such an entry is:

	Debit	Credit
Income tax expense (expense)	xxx	
Accrued income taxes (liability)		xxx

Early Payment Discounts

A key question for the farm accountant is whether to take early payment terms offered by suppliers. This is a common offer when a supplier is short on cash.

The early payment terms offered by suppliers need to be sufficiently lucrative for the accountant to want to pay invoices early, especially when suppliers are offering such generous terms that the farm is effectively earning an inordinately high interest rate in exchange for an early payment.

The term structure used for credit terms is to first state the number of days a supplier is giving its customers from the invoice date in which to take advantage of the early payment credit terms. For example, if a customer is supposed to pay within 10 days without a discount, the terms are "net 10 days," whereas if the customer must pay within 10 days to qualify for a 2% discount, the terms are "2/10." Or, if the customer must pay within 10 days to obtain a 2% discount or can make a normal payment in 30 days, then the terms are stated as "2/10 net 30."

The following table shows some of the more common credit terms, explains what they mean, and also notes the effective interest rate being offered to customers with each one.

Sample Credit Terms

Credit Terms	Explanation	Effective Interest
Net 10	Pay in 10 days	None
Net 30	Pay in 30 days	None
Net EOM 10	Pay within 10 days of month-end	None
1/10 net 30	Take a 1% discount if pay in 10 days, otherwise pay in 30 days	18.2%
2/10 net 30	Take a 2% discount if pay in 10 days, otherwise pay in 30 days	36.7%
1/10 net 60	Take a 1% discount if pay in 10 days, otherwise pay in 60 days	7.3%
2/10 net 60	Take a 2% discount if pay in 10 days, otherwise pay in 60 days	14.7%

In case the accountant is dealing with terms different from those shown in the preceding table, it helps to be aware of the formula for calculating the effective interest rate associated with early payment discount terms. The calculation steps are:

1. Calculate the difference between the payment date for those taking the early payment discount and the date when payment is normally due, and divide it

into 360 days. For example, under "2/10 net 30" terms, the accountant would divide 20 days into 360 to arrive at 18. Use this number to annualize the interest rate calculated in the next step.

2. Subtract the discount percentage from 100% and divide the result into the discount percentage. For example, under "2/10 net 30" terms, divide 2% by 98% to arrive at 0.0204. This is the interest rate being offered through the credit terms.

3. Multiply the result of both calculations together to obtain the annualized interest rate. To conclude the example, multiply 18 by 0.0204 to arrive at an effective annualized interest rate of 36.72%.

Thus, the full calculation for the cost of credit is:

$$(\text{Discount \%} \div (1 - \text{Discount \%})) \times (360 \div (\text{Allowed payment days} - \text{Discount days}))$$

In general, most early payment discounts represent a sufficiently high effective interest rate that the accountant would be foolish to forego them. However, taking such a discount requires that there be sufficient cash on hand.

The simplest way to ensure that all early payment discounts are accepted and paid in a timely manner is to examine every invoice at the point of initial receipt, and set to one side all invoices containing discount offers. This group of invoices containing discounts can then be shifted to a different process flow that emphasizes faster data entry, approval, and payment processing.

If an early payment discount is not taken, be sure to track back through the reasons why the discount was not taken and adjust the processing system to ensure that this does not happen again.

If the farm is paying for relatively large amounts through a credit card, this means that the supplier is being charged a 2% to 3% (or more) fee by the credit card company. In these situations, contact the supplier and offer to instead use a check or ACH payment if the supplier is willing to allow an early payment discount. This approach benefits both parties, since the supplier avoids the credit card fee and the farm earns the amount of the discount.

The Vendor Master File

The vendor master file is the central repository of information about each supplier with which a farm deals. The file is stored within the accounts payable software, and typically contains the following minimum set of information:

- *Supplier identification number.* This is the unique identification number assigned to each supplier by the farm accountant, and which is used to identify the supplier's record in the payables system.
- *Taxpayer identification number.* This is the identification number assigned to a business by the United States government. This information is needed by the farm accountant when completing the year-end Form 1099.

- *Supplier name*. This is the legal name of the supplier, and is commonly used as the pay-to name on check payments to suppliers.
- *Supplier DBA name*. In some cases, a company may have a legal name and a different "doing business as" (or DBA) name by which it is more generally known. This name may instead be used as the pay-to name.
- *Supplier address*. This is the administrative address of the supplier, usually where its billing department is located. This address is used to communicate with the billing department of a supplier.
- *Remit to address*. This is the address to which payments are sent to a supplier.
- *Contact phone number*. This is the phone number of the payables department's contact in the billing department of a supplier, to be used if there are questions about a received billing.
- *Early payment discount code*. If a supplier offers a discount for early payments, enter the terms in this field.
- *1099 flag*. If the farm is required to issue a year-end Form 1099 to a supplier, click on this flag. Doing so will include a supplier in the year-end print run for the Form 1099.
- *Default account*. This is the default expense account to which payments made to the supplier are charged.
- *ACH information*. Separate fields contain room for the supplier's bank routing number and bank account number, as well as the name on the supplier's bank account.

Vendor Master File Usage

The vendor master file is a central component of many payables activities, which is why a high level of record accuracy is needed. Here are several examples of situations in which the file is used:

- *Invoice receipt*. The farm accountant receives an invoice from a supplier. To enter the invoice in the accounting system for payment, the accountant first does a lookup of supplier names in the vendor master file, to find the correct record. Once this record is selected, the system automatically links the new invoice record with the supplier address and early payment discount information (if any) in the vendor master file. The only information that enters the invoice record from the invoice is the invoice date, invoice number, and total amount payable.
- *Supplier payment*. When it is time to pay suppliers, the accounting system draws the amount payable from the invoice record, and the pay-to name and address from the vendor master file. If an ACH payment is being made, the supplier's bank account information is also drawn from the vendor master file.
- *1099 reporting*. At year-end, the farm may have to issue a completed Form 1099 for certain suppliers. The program in the accounting system that generates these reports uses the 1099 flag in the vendor master file to decide

whether a report should be issued at all, and uses the supplier address information and taxpayer identification number in the file to populate the report.

In short, the vendor master file contains a large amount of information about suppliers that is central to the efficient functioning of the farm accountant.

A supplier may not necessarily be set up with a record in the vendor master file. This is most likely to be the case when there is an expectation that a supplier will only be used once. In this case, it may be more efficient to enter all necessary payment information in a separate data entry form in the payables software. The result will be a single invoice record that contains all information needed to pay a supplier. If such an entity were to become a more frequent supplier with regular billings, it would then make more sense to create a unique record for it in the vendor master file.

Tip: It might be tempting to create a vendor master file record for every supplier, no matter how infrequently the farm uses the supplier. However, this creates an inordinate number of records in the file, which makes it more difficult to manage.

Supplier Naming Conventions

It is important to avoid creating a new record in the vendor master file for suppliers that already have an existing record. Otherwise, the farm accountant will assign some supplier invoices to one version of a master file record and some invoices to a different version. This can lead to the following situations:

- *Duplicate payment.* An invoice is initially submitted and recorded under one version of the supplier record; the invoice payment is late in arriving, so the supplier sends a duplicate invoice, which is recorded under a different version of the supplier record. The result is that the second invoice is not flagged by the software as being a duplicate invoice, so the farm pays the supplier twice.
- *Incomplete records.* The accounting system reveals an incomplete list of billings from a supplier, since some billings are linked to a different supplier record.
- *Incorrect 1099.* A year-end Form 1099 is completed that does not contain the total amount paid to a supplier, since the payments are split among different records.
- *Missing address update.* A supplier submits an address change, but the change is only updated on one of its record versions, resulting in some old invoices being paid to an old pay-to address.

To avoid these problems, it is necessary to create and follow a rigidly-defined naming convention. A naming convention sets forth rules for how to create a supplier identification number. For example, the name of a new supplier for a farm is The Scot's Guard Herbicides. When developing an identification number, the following problems arise:

- Should the identification number start with "The" or with "Scot's"?

- Should the identification number include the apostrophe in the "Scot's" part of the name?
- How much of this long supplier name should be included in the identification number?

The usual naming convention would drop "The" and the apostrophe from the identification number, and probably truncate the name after five or six characters. By employing these rules, the supplier identification number would become either SCOTS (five characters) or SCOTSG (six characters).

How should a naming convention deal with several suppliers whose names begin with the same characters? The convention usually allows for the sequential numbering of these additional suppliers. For example, the first supplier that a farm has is The Scot's Guard Herbicides, so the preceding naming convention indicates that the supplier identification number should be SCOTS001. A year later, the farm takes on a supplier with the somewhat similar name of Scot's Silo Service. Under the terms of the naming convention, the identification number assigned to this supplier will be SCOTS002.

There may be a need for a number of additional naming conventions to deal with unusual supplier names, such as:

- Eliminate all spaces from supplier names. For example, Jones and Smith could be interpreted as JONESAN001.
- Drop all periods from a name. For example, I.D.C. Corporation could be interpreted as IDCCO001.
- Use an ampersand (&) instead of "and" in a name. To return to the preceding Jones and Smith supplier name, it could be interpreted as JONES&S. Doing so leaves more room to introduce additional characters that could uniquely identify a supplier.
- Use the last name of an individual. For example, the farm pays a private contractor named John Arbuckle. There are many contractors named John, so the identification number instead uses the last name to derive ARBUC001.

The Payables Filing System

The payables function is one of the largest generators of paperwork in a farm. It should be organized to meet the following two goals:

- To make documents easily accessible for payment purposes
- To make documents easily accessible for auditors

The second requirement, to have paperwork available for auditors, does not just refer to the auditors who examine the company's financial statements at year-end. In addition, the local government may send use tax auditors who will also review the records. Consider maintaining the following systems of records to meet the preceding needs:

- *Supplier files.* There should be one file for each supplier that has been paid within the past year. Within each file, staple all paid invoices and related documents to the remittance advice for each paid check. These checks should be filed by date, with the most recent payment in front.
- *Unpaid invoices file.* There should be a separate file of unpaid invoices, which is usually sorted alphabetically by the name of the supplier. If there is more than one unpaid invoice for a supplier, sort them by date for each supplier.
- *Unmatched documents file.* If the company is using three-way matching, have separate files for unmatched invoices, purchase orders, and receiving documentation. Three-way matching refers to comparing a supplier invoice to an authorizing purchase order and receiving documentation before paying the supplier.

Tip: It is not necessary to maintain a separate supplier folder for every supplier. If a supplier only issues invoices a few times a year, include them in an "Other" folder that applies to a letter range of suppliers. For example, there may be an "Other A-C" folder, followed by an "Other D-F" folder, and so forth. Review these "Other" folders periodically, extract the invoices of any suppliers that are generating an increasing volume of invoices, and prepare separate folders for these suppliers.

Government Reporting

The key government reporting requirement for payables is the provision of the Form 1099 to the government following the end of each calendar year. In this section, we describe the contents of this form, the use of the Form W-9 to obtain the identification information used on the Form 1099, and several related topics.

The Form 1099-MISC

The Form 1099-MISC, "Miscellaneous Information," contains the aggregate amount of cash payments made to a supplier in the preceding calendar year. The IRS uses this document to confirm the amount of income that each supplier reports on its annual tax return. Depending on the type of payment made, it is usually not necessary to issue the form if the cumulative cash payments to a supplier for the full calendar year are less than $600. The form must also be filed for any person from whom you withheld any federal income tax under the backup withholding rules, no matter how small the amount may be.

Note: Personal payments are not reported on the Form 1099-MISC, only payments made in the course of your farm business.

The form is to be sent to the payee by January 31 and filed with the Internal Revenue Service (IRS) by February 28 (or by March 31 if filing electronically[1]). The filing period can be extended 30 days by requesting an extension on IRS Form 8809 (which is available as an on-line form). The form copies are distributed as follows:

- Copy A to the IRS
- Copy B to the recipient (supplier)
- Copy C to be retained by the company
- Copy 1 to the state tax department
- Copy 2 to the recipient (supplier) to file with its state income tax return

There are several exceptions to the requirement to issue a Form 1099-MISC. All of the following do *not* require reporting (this is a partial list):

- Payments made to corporations, including S corporations
- Payments for merchandise, telegrams, telephone, freight, and storage
- Payments of rent to real estate agents or property managers
- Wages paid to employees
- Business travel allowances paid to employees
- The cost of life insurance protection
- Payments to a tax-exempt organization
- Payments to the United States, a state, a U.S. possession, or a foreign government
- Cancelled debts that are reportable on the Form 1099-C

A sample Form 1099-MISC follows.

---

[1] Electronic filing is required when filing 100 or more 1099 forms. See IRS Publication 1220 for more information about electronic filing.

Sample Form 1099-MISC

Explanations of the key boxes on the form are noted in the following table.

Contents of Key 1099-MISC Fields

Box ID	Description
Box 1	Rent – Includes real estate rentals paid for office space, unless they were paid to a real estate agent. Also includes machine rentals and pasture rentals. The minimum reporting threshold is $600.
Box 2	Royalties – Includes gross royalty payments, such as from oil, gas, and other mineral properties, as well as from patents, copyrights, trade names, and trademarks. The minimum reporting threshold is $10.
Box 3	Other income – Includes other income of at least $600 that is not reportable under any of the other boxes on the form. Includes the fair market value of merchandise won on game shows, as well as payments to individuals for participating in a medical research study and punitive damage payments.
Box 4	Federal income tax withheld – Includes any backup withholdings made on payments to suppliers. This is most likely when suppliers have not furnished you with taxpayer identification numbers.

Box ID	Description
Box 6	Medical and health care payments – Includes payments to each physician or other provider of medical or health care services. The minimum reporting threshold is $600. Typical payments include charges for injections, drugs, dentures, and similar items. This does not include payments made to a tax-exempt hospital or an extended care facility.
Box 9	Crop insurance proceeds – Includes payments made by insurance companies to farmers. The minimum reporting threshold is $600.
Box 10	Gross proceeds paid to an attorney – Includes amounts paid to an attorney for legal services. The minimum reporting threshold is $600.

When submitting 1099s to the federal government, also include a Form 1096 transmittal return, which is essentially a cover letter that identifies the entity providing the forms. A sample Form 1096 follows.

Sample Form 1096

The Form W-9

A farm needs accurate identification information about each of its suppliers before it can submit the Form 1099 to the government. To collect this information, have all suppliers submit a Form W-9, Request for Taxpayer Identification Number and Certification. A sample Form W-9 follows.

Sample Form W-9

| Form **W-9** (Rev. October 2018) Department of the Treasury Internal Revenue Service | **Request for Taxpayer Identification Number and Certification** ▶ Go to *www.irs.gov/FormW9* for instructions and the latest information. | Give Form to the requester. Do not send to the IRS. |

1 Name (as shown on your income tax return). Name is required on this line; do not leave this line blank.

2 Business name/disregarded entity name, if different from above

3 Check appropriate box for federal tax classification of the person whose name is entered on line 1. Check only **one** of the following seven boxes.

☐ Individual/sole proprietor or single-member LLC   ☐ C Corporation   ☐ S Corporation   ☐ Partnership   ☐ Trust/estate

☐ Limited liability company. Enter the tax classification (C=C corporation, S=S corporation, P=Partnership) ▶ _____

Note: Check the appropriate box in the line above for the tax classification of the single-member owner. Do not check LLC if the LLC is classified as a single-member LLC that is disregarded from the owner unless the owner of the LLC is another LLC that is **not** disregarded from the owner for U.S. federal tax purposes. Otherwise, a single-member LLC that is disregarded from the owner should check the appropriate box for the tax classification of its owner.

☐ Other (see instructions) ▶

4 Exemptions (codes apply only to certain entities, not individuals; see instructions on page 3):

Exempt payee code (if any) _____

Exemption from FATCA reporting code (if any) _____

(Applies to accounts maintained outside the U.S.)

5 Address (number, street, and apt. or suite no.) See instructions.

6 City, state, and ZIP code

Requester's name and address (optional)

7 List account number(s) here (optional)

Part I   Taxpayer Identification Number (TIN)

Enter your TIN in the appropriate box. The TIN provided must match the name given on line 1 to avoid backup withholding. For individuals, this is generally your social security number (SSN). However, for a resident alien, sole proprietor, or disregarded entity, see the instructions for Part I, later. For other entities, it is your employer identification number (EIN). If you do not have a number, see *How to get a TIN*, later.

Note: If the account is in more than one name, see the instructions for line 1. Also see *What Name and Number To Give the Requester* for guidelines on whose number to enter.

Social security number

or

Employer identification number

Part II   Certification

Under penalties of perjury, I certify that:

1. The number shown on this form is my correct taxpayer identification number (or I am waiting for a number to be issued to me); and
2. I am not subject to backup withholding because: (a) I am exempt from backup withholding, or (b) I have not been notified by the Internal Revenue Service (IRS) that I am subject to backup withholding as a result of a failure to report all interest or dividends, or (c) the IRS has notified me that I am no longer subject to backup withholding; and
3. I am a U.S. citizen or other U.S. person (defined below); and
4. The FATCA code(s) entered on this form (if any) indicating that I am exempt from FATCA reporting is correct.

Certification instructions. You must cross out item 2 above if you have been notified by the IRS that you are currently subject to backup withholding because you have failed to report all interest and dividends on your tax return. For real estate transactions, item 2 does not apply. For mortgage interest paid, acquisition or abandonment of secured property, cancellation of debt, contributions to an individual retirement arrangement (IRA), and generally, payments other than interest and dividends, you are not required to sign the certification, but you must provide your correct TIN. See the instructions for Part II, later.

Sign Here   Signature of U.S. person ▶   Date ▶

It is a good practice to have the Form W-9 updated on an annual basis, in order to have the most recent mailing address on file for each supplier. Doing so also warns of any organizational changes in a supplier. However, this can be difficult if there are many suppliers. Usually, a simple e-mail notice to each supplier to ask for a revised Form W-9 if there have been any informational changes is considered sufficient.

Summary

The farm accountant must deal with accounts payable in a highly organized manner. Otherwise, there is a good chance that suppliers will be paid too late, not at all, or more than once – none of which are good for the reputation of the farm. When these situations occur on a regular basis, suppliers are more likely to withdraw credit, leaving a farm to pay up-front with cash. Consequently, payables is the first place in which to create rigid procedures, filing standards, and calendars of activities.

Chapter 11
Debt Accounting

Introduction

The owners of a farm may not be able to support its operations entirely from their own resources, and so must obtain debt from lenders. Doing so can boost their return on investment, if the amount of profit generated by the farm exceeds the amount of interest expense associated with the debt.

The accounting for debt is not especially difficult, especially if the farm is a smaller family-run affair that only has a few loans outstanding. Also, the accounting entries needed are fairly simple. However, it is necessary to determine the interest component of each debt payment, so that the farm properly presents in its balance sheet the correct amount of remaining debt outstanding.

In this chapter, we address the classification of and accounting for debt, as well as the concept of the amortization schedule and the need to periodically reconcile the debt account.

Basic Debt Accounting

Debt is defined as an amount owed for funds borrowed. This may take a variety of forms, such as:

- Credit card debt, which can either be paid off each month or carried forward in exchange for a high interest rate.
- A line of credit, which is used to meet short-term needs, and which is usually limited to the amount of collateral that the borrower has available to guarantee repayment. A line of credit balance may fluctuate up or down during a year, and is expected to be paid off at least once a year.
- A promissory note, which is a fixed sum that a farm borrows and then commits to pay back over time, in accordance with a fixed repayment schedule.

There are several issues that the farm accountant must be aware of when accounting for debt. The initial issue is how to classify the debt in the accounting records. Here are the main areas to be concerned with:

- If the debt is payable within one year, record the debt in a short-term debt account; this is a liability account. The typical line of credit is payable within one year, and so is classified as short-term debt.
- If the debt is payable in more than one year, record the debt in a long-term debt account; this is a liability account.
- If a loan agreement contains a clause stating that the lender can demand payment at any time, classify the debt as a current liability. This is the case even

if there is no expectation that the lender will demand payment within the current year.

- If the debt is in the form of a credit card statement, this is typically handled as an account payable, and so is simply recorded through the accounts payable module in the farm's accounting software (see the Payables Accounting chapter).

The next debt accounting issue is how to determine the amount of interest expense associated with debt. This is usually quite easy, since the lender includes the amount of the interest expense on its periodic billing statements to the farm. In the case of a line of credit, the borrower is probably required to maintain its primary checking account with the lending bank, so the bank simply deducts the interest from the checking account once a month. This amount is usually identified as an interest charge on the monthly bank statement, so one can easily identify and record it as part of the monthly bank reconciliation adjustments. Alternatively, the lender may provide an amortization schedule to the borrower, which states the proportions of interest expense and loan repayment that will comprise each subsequent payment made to the lender. See the next section for a description of an amortization schedule.

As an alternative, the amount of interest expense can be calculated with the following formula:

$$\text{Outstanding debt} \times \text{Interest rate} \times \text{Days outstanding} = \text{Interest expense}$$

For example, the owners of a farm have taken out a $200,000 loan at an interest rate of 8%. At the end of one month, the related interest expense is:

$$\$200,000 \text{ Debt} \times 8\% \text{ Interest} \times 1/12 \text{ Year} = \$1,333.33$$

A lender may require a small commitment fee for the unused balance of a line of credit. This is essentially another form of interest expense. For example, a farm manager negotiates for a $500,000 line of credit, and is currently using $380,000 of this amount, leaving $120,000 unused. The farm's lender charges a ¼% fee on the unused balance each month, which is $300 (calculated as $120,000 unused funds × 0.0025).

The next issue is how to account for the various debt-related transactions. They are as follows:

- *Initial loan.* When a loan is first taken out, debit the cash account and credit either the short-term debt account or long-term debt account, depending on the nature of the loan. For example, a farm borrows $1,000,000. The entry is:

	Debit	Credit
Cash [asset account]	1,000,000	
Long-term debt [liability account]		1,000,000

- *Interest payment.* If there is no immediate loan repayment, with only interest being paid, then the entry is a debit to the interest expense account and a credit to the cash account. For example, the interest rate on the $1,000,000 just described is 7%, with payments due at the end of each year. After one year, the entry is:

	Debit	Credit
Interest expense [expense account]	70,000	
Cash [asset account]		70,000

- *Commitment fee.* If a portion of the funds set aside by a lender for a line of credit is unused, a commitment fee may be charged to the borrower. The entry is a debit to the interest expense account and a credit to the cash account. For example, the annual ¼% commitment fee on $100,000 of an unused line of credit is $250. The entry is:

	Debit	Credit
Interest expense [expense account]	250	
Cash [asset account]		250

- *Mixed payment.* If a payment is being made that includes both interest expense and a loan repayment, debit the interest expense account, debit the applicable loan liability account, and credit the cash account. For example, a $5,000 loan payment is comprised of $4,300 of interest expense and $700 of loan repayment. The entry is:

	Debit	Credit
Interest expense [expense account]	4,300	
Short-term debt [liability account]	700	
Cash [asset account]		5,000

- *Final payment.* If there is a final balloon payment where most or all of the debt is repaid, debit the applicable loan liability account and credit the cash account. For example, a farm has been paying nothing but interest on a $500,000 loan for the past four years, and now repays the entire loan balance. The entry is:

	Debit	Credit
Short-term debt [liability account]	500,000	
Cash [asset account]		500,000

The Amortization Schedule

An amortization schedule is a table that states the periodic payments to be made as part of a loan agreement, and which notes the following information on each line of the table:

- Payment number
- Payment due date
- Payment total
- Interest component of payment
- Principal component of payment
- Ending principal balance remaining

Thus, the calculation on each line of the amortization schedule is designed to arrive at the ending principal balance for each period, for which the calculation is:

Beginning principal balance - (Payment total - Interest expense) = Ending principal balance

The amortization schedule is extremely useful for accounting for each payment in a promissory note, since it separates the interest and principal components of each payment. The schedule is also useful for modeling how the remaining loan liability will vary if payments are accelerated or delayed, or if their size is altered. An amortization schedule can also encompass balloon payments (where the entire principal is paid at the end of the loan period) and even negative amortization situations where the principal balance increases over time.

A sample amortization schedule follows, where a farm has taken on a $50,000 loan that is to be repaid with five annual payments, using an interest rate of 8%. Note how the proportion of interest expense to the total payment made rapidly declines, until there is almost no interest expense remaining in the final payment. The schedule also notes the total interest expense associated with the loan.

Sample Amortization Schedule

Year	Beginning Loan Balance	Loan Payment	8% Interest	Loan Repayment	Ending Loan Balance
1	$50,000	$12,523	$4,000	$8,523	$41,477
2	41,477	12,523	3,318	9,205	32,272
3	32,272	12,523	2,582	9,941	22,331
4	22,331	12,523	1,786	10,737	11,594
5	11,594	12,522	928	11,594	0
		$62,614	$12,614	$50,000	

* Note: The Year 5 payment was reduced by $1 to offset the effects of rounding.

Reconciling the Debt Account

It is essential to periodically compare the remaining loan balance reported by the lender to the balance reported on the books of the farm. It is entirely possible that there will be a difference, for which there are usually two reasons. They are:

- The loan payments made by the farm to the lender arrived either earlier or later than the payment due date. This alters the amount of interest expense charged to the farm.
- The most recent loan payment made by the farm to the lender is still in transit to the lender, or has not yet been recorded by the lender in its accounting system.

If there is a difference, contact the lender and determine the nature of the difference. If the interest charge recognized by the lender varies from the amount recognized by the farm accountant, alter the farm's interest expense to match the amount recognized by the lender. If the difference is due to a payment in transit, no adjustment to the accounting records needs to be made.

The reason why this reconciliation is so necessary is that the farm's auditors will contact the lender at the end of the year to confirm with them the amount owed by the farm. If the auditors discover a difference, they will require the farm accountant to adjust the farm's loan records.

Summary

Though debt accounting should not be especially difficult, we must emphasize the need to reconcile the debt account at regular intervals. This is an area in which the amounts of interest recognized by the lender and borrower can easily diverge, resulting in notable differences. It is better to locate and eliminate these differences prior to year-end, rather than having the auditors discover them.

Some farms have a number of loans outstanding, perhaps with separate loans to pay for various types of equipment, land purchases, or construction projects. If so, the amount of debt that a farm is carrying on its books may be its single largest obligation, and so warrants the most attention to ensure that it is correctly recorded.

Chapter 12
Income Taxes

Introduction

If a farm generates a profit, it will probably be necessary to record income tax expense that is a percentage of the profit. However, the calculation of income tax is not so simple, since it may be based on a number of adjustments to net income that are allowed by the taxing authorities. The result can be remarkably complex tax measurements. In this chapter, we describe the general concepts of income tax accounting, as well as the calculation of the appropriate tax rate, the evaluation of tax positions, how to treat deferred taxes, and how to record taxes in interim periods.

Overview of Income Taxes

Before delving into the income taxes topic, we must clarify several concepts that are essential to understanding the related accounting. The concepts are:

- *Temporary differences.* A farm may record an asset or liability at one value for financial reporting purposes, while maintaining a separate record of a different value for tax purposes. The difference is caused by the tax recognition policies of taxing authorities, who may require the deferral or acceleration of certain items for tax reporting purposes. These differences are temporary, since the assets will eventually be recovered and the liabilities settled, at which point the differences will be terminated. A difference that results in a taxable amount in a later period is called a *taxable temporary difference*, while a difference that results in a deductible amount in a later period is called a *deductible temporary difference*. Examples of temporary differences are:
  - Revenues or gains that are taxable either prior to or after they are recognized in the financial statements. For example, an allowance for doubtful accounts may not be immediately tax deductible, but instead must be deferred until specific receivables are declared bad debts.
  - Expenses or losses that are tax deductible either prior to or after they are recognized in the financial statements. For example, some fixed assets are tax deductible at once, but can only be recognized through long-term depreciation in the financial statements.
  - Assets whose tax basis is reduced by investment tax credits.

EXAMPLE

In its most recent year of operations, Table Mountain Farm earns $250,000. Table also has $30,000 of taxable temporary differences and $80,000 of deductible temporary differences. Based on this information, Table's taxable income in the current year is calculated as:

$250,000 Profit - $30,000 Taxable temporary differences
+ $80,000 Deductible temporary differences

= $300,000 Taxable profit

- *Carrybacks and carryforwards.* A farm may find that it has more tax deductions or tax credits (from an operating loss) than it can use in the current year's tax return. If so, it has the option of offsetting these amounts against the taxable income or tax liabilities (respectively) of the tax returns in earlier periods, or in future periods. Carrying these amounts back to the tax returns of prior periods is always more valuable, since the farm can apply for a tax refund at once. Thus, these excess tax deductions or tax credits are carried back first, with any remaining amounts being reserved for use in future periods. Carryforwards eventually expire if not used within a certain number of years. A farm should recognize a receivable for the amount of taxes paid in prior years that are refundable due to a carryback. A deferred tax asset can be realized for a carryforward, but possibly with an offsetting valuation allowance that is based on the probability that some portion of the carryforward will not be realized.

EXAMPLE

Spastic Farm has created $100,000 of deferred tax assets through the diligent generation of losses for the past five years. Based on the farm's poor results, the farm manager believes it is more likely than not that there will be inadequate profits (if any) against which the deferred tax assets can be offset. Accordingly, Spastic recognizes a valuation allowance in the amount of $100,000 that fully offsets the deferred tax assets.

- *Deferred tax liabilities and assets.* When there are temporary differences, the result can be deferred tax assets and deferred tax liabilities, which represent the change in taxes payable or refundable in future periods.

EXAMPLE

Missionary Ridge Farm has recorded the following carrying amount and tax basis information for certain of its assets and liabilities:

(000s)	Carrying Amount	Tax Basis	Temporary Difference
Accounts receivable	$12,000	$12,250	-$250
Prepaid expenses	350	350	0
Livestock	8,000	8,000	0
Fixed assets	17,300	14,900	2,400
Accounts payable	3,700	3,700	0
Totals	$41,350	$39,200	$2,150

In the table, Missionary Ridge has included a reserve for bad debts in its accounts receivable figure, which is not allowed for tax purposes. Also, the farm applied an accelerated form of depreciation to its fixed assets for tax purposes and straight-line depreciation for its financial reporting. These items account for the total temporary difference between the carrying amount and tax basis of the items shown in the table.

All of these factors can result in complex calculations to arrive at the appropriate income tax information to recognize and report in the financial statements.

Accounting for Income Taxes

Despite the complexity inherent in income taxes, the essential accounting in this area is derived from the need to recognize two items, which are:

- *Current year.* The recognition of a tax liability or tax asset, based on the estimated amount of income taxes payable or refundable for the current year.
- *Future years.* The recognition of a deferred tax liability or tax asset, based on the estimated effects in future years of carryforwards and temporary differences.

Based on the preceding points, the general accounting for income taxes is noted in the following table.

Basic Accounting for Income Taxes

+/-	Create a tax liability for estimated taxes payable, and/or create a tax asset for tax refunds, that relate to the current or prior years
+/-	Create a deferred tax liability for estimated future taxes payable, and/or create a deferred tax asset for estimated future tax refunds, that can be attributed to temporary differences and carryforwards
=	Total income tax expense in the period

Tax Positions

A tax position is a stance taken by a farm in its tax return that measures tax assets and liabilities, and which results in the permanent reduction or temporary deferral of income taxes. When constructing the proper accounting for a tax position, the farm accountant follows these steps:

1. Evaluate whether the tax position taken has merit, based on the tax regulations.
2. If the tax position has merit, measure the amount that can be recognized in the financial statements.
3. Determine the probability and amount of settlement with the taxing authorities. Recognition should only be made when it is more likely than not (i.e., more than 50% probability) that the farm's tax position will be sustained once it has been examined by the governing tax authorities.
4. Recognize the tax position, if warranted.

Tip: Given the large financial impact of some tax positions, it makes sense to obtain an outside opinion of a proposed position by a tax expert, and document the results of that review thoroughly. This is helpful not only if the position is reviewed by the taxing authorities, but also when it is reviewed by the farm's auditors.

EXAMPLE

Armadillo Ranch takes a tax position on an issue and determines that the position qualifies for recognition, and so should be recognized. The following table shows the estimated possible outcomes of the tax position, along with their associated probabilities:

Possible Outcome	Probability of Occurrence	Cumulative Probability
$250,000	5%	5%
200,000	20%	25%
150,000	40%	65%
100,000	20%	85%
50,000	10%	95%
0	5%	100%

Since the benefit amount just beyond the 50% threshold level is $150,000, Armadillo should recognize a tax benefit of $150,000.

If the farm accountant initially concludes that the probability of a tax position being sustained is less than 50%, he should not initially recognize the tax position. However, he can recognize the position at a later date if the probability increases to be in excess of 50%, or if the tax position is settled through interaction with the taxing authorities, or the statute of limitations keeps the taxing authorities from challenging the tax position. If the farm accountant subsequently concludes that he will change a tax position previously taken, he should recognize the effect of the change in the period in which he alters the tax position. A farm can also derecognize a tax position that it had previously recognized if the probability of the tax position being sustained drops below 50%.

EXAMPLE

Armadillo Ranch takes a tax position under which it accelerates the depreciation of certain farm equipment well beyond the normally-allowed taxable rate, resulting in a deferred tax liability after three years of $120,000.

After three years, a tax court ruling convinces Armadillo's manager that its tax position is untenable. Consequently, the farm accountant recognizes a tax liability for the $120,000 temporary difference. At the farm's current 35% tax rate, this results in increased taxes of $42,000 and the elimination of the temporary difference.

Deferred Tax Expense

Deferred tax expense is the net change in the deferred tax liabilities and tax assets of a farm during a period of time. The amount of deferred taxes should be compiled for each reporting period, which requires that the farm accountant complete the following steps:

1. Identify the existing temporary differences and carryforwards.
2. Determine the deferred tax liability amount for those temporary differences that are taxable, using the applicable tax rate.
3. Determine the deferred tax asset amount for those temporary differences that are deductible, as well as any operating loss carryforwards, using the applicable tax rate.
4. Determine the deferred tax asset amount for any carryforwards involving tax credits.
5. Create a valuation allowance for the deferred tax assets if there is a more than 50% probability that the farm will not realize some portion of these assets. Any changes to this allowance are to be recorded on the income statement. The need for a valuation allowance is especially likely if a farm has a history of letting various carryforwards expire unused, or it expects to incur losses in the next few years.

Applicable Tax Rate

If the applicable tax law has graduated tax rates and the graduated rates significantly affect the average tax rate paid, use the average tax rate that applies to the estimated annual taxable income in those periods when deferred tax liabilities are settled or deferred tax assets are realized. If a farm earns such a large amount of income that the graduated rate is not significantly different from the top-tier tax rate, use the top-tier rate for the estimation of annual taxable income.

Interim Reporting

If a farm reports its financial results during interim reporting periods (such as monthly or quarterly financial statements), it must report income taxes in those interim reports. In general, the proper accounting is to report income taxes using an estimated effective tax rate in all of the interim periods. However, the application of this general principle varies somewhat as noted below:

- *Ordinary income.* Calculate the income tax on ordinary income at the estimated annual effective tax rate.
- *Other items.* Calculate and recognize the income tax on all items other than ordinary income at the rates that are applicable when the items occur. This means that the related tax effect is recognized in the period in which the underlying items occur.

The following factors apply to the determination of the estimated annual effective tax rate:

- The tax benefit associated with any applicable loss carryforward
- The tax effect of any valuation allowance used to offset the deferred tax asset
- Anticipated investment tax credits (for the amount expected to be used within the year)
- Foreign tax rates
- Capital gains rates
- The effects of new tax legislation, though only after it has been passed

EXAMPLE

In the current fiscal year, Armadillo Ranch anticipates $1,000,000 of ordinary income, to which will be applied the statutory tax rate of 40%, which will result in an income tax expense of $400,000. Armadillo also expects to take advantage of a $100,000 investment tax credit. Thus, the effective tax rate for the year is expected to be 30%, which is calculated as $300,000 of net taxes, divided by $1,000,000 of ordinary income.

The estimated tax rate is to be reviewed at the end of each interim period and adjusted as necessary, based on the latest estimates of taxable income to be reported for the full year. If it is not possible to derive an estimated tax rate, it may be necessary to instead use the actual effective tax rate for the year to date.

If the estimated tax rate is revised in an interim period from the rate used in a prior period, use the new estimate to derive the year-to-date tax on ordinary income for all interim periods to date.

The tax benefit associated with a loss recorded in an earlier interim period may not be recognized, on the grounds that it is less than 50% probable that the benefit will be realized. If so, do not recognize any income tax for ordinary income reported in subsequent periods until the unrecognized tax benefit associated with the original loss has been offset with income.

EXAMPLE

Through its first two quarters, Mellow Meadows Farm has experienced losses of $400,000 and $600,000. The farm accountant concludes that it is more likely than not that the tax benefit associated with these losses will not be realized. The farm then earns profits in the third and fourth quarters, resulting in the following application of taxes at the statutory 40% rate:

| (000s) | Ordinary Income | | Income Tax | | |
	Current Period	Cumulative	Cumulative Tax (40%)	Less Previous Amount	Tax Provision
Quarter 1	-$400	-$400	--	---	--
Quarter 2	-600	-1,000	--	---	--
Quarter 3	1,100	100	$40	---	$40
Quarter 4	300	400	160	$40	120
Totals	$400				$160

If a farm records a loss during an interim period, the farm accountant should only recognize the tax effects of the loss (i.e., a corresponding reduction in taxes) when there is an expectation that the tax reduction will be realized later in the year, or will be recognized as a deferred tax asset by year-end. This recognition may occur later in the year, if it later becomes more likely than not that the tax effects of the loss can be realized.

EXAMPLE

Mellow Meadows Farm has a history of recording losses in its first and second quarters, after which revenue increases during the summer and winter. In the first half of the current year, Mellow records a $1,000,000 loss, but expects a $2,000,000 profit in the final half of the year. Based on the farm's history of seasonal sales, realization of the tax loss appears to be more likely than not, so Mellow's accountant records the tax effect of the loss in the first half of the year.

Summary

Many farm accountants consider income tax accounting to be an area best left to a tax specialist, who churns through the information provided and creates a set of tax-related journal entries. While this approach should result in accurate tax accounting, it does not give the farm manager a good view of how his actions are affecting the taxes the farm is paying – instead, the tax accounting function is treated as a black box whose contents are unknown to all, save the tax specialist who guards it.

A better approach is to engage the farm manager in tax planning by providing instruction on the essential tax issues that can be impacted by various operating decisions. Even if the manager does not become conversant at a detailed level in how his actions impact income taxes, he will at least know when to call in a tax expert for advice. Thus, a certain amount of transparency in the tax area can improve the results of a farm.

Chapter 13
Derivatives and Hedging Transactions

Introduction

Prices for farm products change due to variations in the supply or demand fundamentals for each product. Periods of tight supplies typically lead to high prices. Farmers do not often have stored grain or marketable livestock on hand at a time when prices are high. Hedging is a way to lock in prices in higher-priced periods.

Hedging is *the* most complex accounting topic that applies to agricultural transactions. There are two key concepts in the accounting for hedges. The first is that ongoing changes in the fair value of derivatives (as explained in the next section) not used in hedging arrangements are generally recognized in earnings at once. The second is that ongoing changes in the fair value of derivatives and the hedged items with which they are paired may be parked in other comprehensive income for a period of time, thereby removing them from the basic earnings reported by a farm. In the following sections, we build upon these concepts by addressing the nature of derivatives and hedges, other comprehensive income, and the details of the various types of derivative and hedge accounting.

The Nature of a Derivative

A *financial instrument* is a document that has monetary value or which establishes an obligation to pay. Examples of financial instruments are cash, accounts receivable, loans, bonds, equity securities, and accounts payable. A *derivative* is a financial instrument that has the following characteristics:

- It is a financial instrument or a contract that requires either a small or no initial investment;
- There is at least one *notional amount* (the face value of a financial instrument, which is used to make calculations based on that amount) or payment provision;
- It can be settled *net*, which is a payment that reflects the net difference between the ending positions of the two parties; and
- Its value changes in relation to a change in an *underlying*, which is a variable, such as an interest rate, exchange rate, credit rating, or commodity price, that is used to determine the settlement of a derivative instrument. The value of a derivative can even change in conjunction with the weather.

Examples of derivatives include the following:

- *Call option*. An agreement that gives the holder the right, but not the obligation, to *buy* shares, bonds, commodities, or other assets at a pre-determined price within a pre-defined time period.
- *Put option*. An agreement that gives the holder the right, but not the obligation, to *sell* shares, bonds, commodities, or other assets at a pre-determined price within a pre-defined time period.
- *Forward*. An agreement to buy or sell an asset at a pre-determined price as of a future date. This is a highly customizable derivative, which is not traded on an exchange.
- *Futures*. An agreement to buy or sell an asset at a pre-determined price as of a future date. This is a standardized agreement, so that they can be more easily traded on a futures exchange.

In essence, a derivative constitutes a bet that something will increase or decrease. A derivative can be used to avoid risk.

When entering into a derivative arrangement, neither party to the arrangement pays the entire value of the instrument up front. Instead, the net difference between the obligations of the two parties is tracked over time, with final settlement being based on the net difference between the final positions of the parties when the instrument is terminated. Also, there is no delivery or receipt of any non-financial item. This arrangement is referred to as *net settlement*.

By minimizing the need for an up-front investment, a farm can enter into a derivative arrangement at minimal cost. This makes the use of derivatives much more cost-effective than would be the case if they were paid for up front and in full.

The value of a derivative changes in concert with the variability of the underlying on which it is based. For example, if a derivative is tied to a benchmark interest rate and there is a minimal expectation that the interest rate will change during the life of the derivative, then the seller of the derivative bears little risk of having to pay out, and so will accept a low price for the derivative. Conversely, if there is an expectation of major changes in the underlying, the risk that the seller will have to pay out increases, so the seller will require a much higher price for the derivative.

The Nature of a Hedge

Hedging is a risk reduction technique, under which an entity uses a derivative or similar instrument to offset future changes in the fair value or cash flows of an asset or liability. The ideal outcome of a hedge is when the distribution of probable outcomes is reduced, so that the size of any potential loss is reduced. The following exhibit shows the effect of hedging on the range of possible outcomes.

Impact of Hedging on Risk Outcome

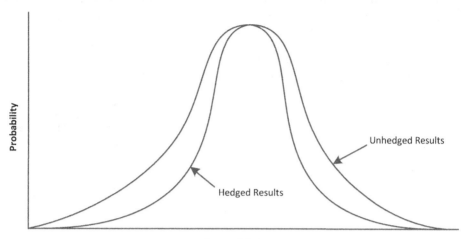

In agriculture, a hedged item is usually stored crop inventory, growing crops, future crops, or livestock that is being raised or will be raised.

Hedge effectiveness is the amount of the changes in the fair value or cash flows of a hedged item that are offset by changes in the fair value or cash flows of a hedging instrument. A highly effective hedging transaction is one in which the net effect of a pairing of a hedged item and a hedging instrument is close to zero.

Other Comprehensive Income

In the following sections, we will refer to the recordation of certain hedging results in other comprehensive income (OCI). We explained OCI in the Investment Accounting chapter, but will do so here again, with a slant toward how OCI is used in the accounting for hedges.

The intent behind the concept of comprehensive income is to report on all changes in the equity of a business, other than those involving the owners of the business. Not all of these transactions appear in the income statement, so comprehensive income is needed to provide a broader view. Comprehensive income is comprised of net income and other comprehensive income. For the purposes of this discussion, other comprehensive income is comprised of gains and losses on derivative instruments that are cash flow hedges. We will address cash flow hedges shortly.

If the items initially stated in OCI are later displayed as part of net income (typically because the transactions have been settled), this is essentially a reclassification out of the OCI classification. Otherwise, the items will be double-counted within comprehensive income. For example, an unrealized gain on an investment is initially recorded within OCI and is then sold, at which point the gain is realized and shifted from OCI to net income. In short, there is a continual shifting of items from OCI to net income over time.

Items of comprehensive income must be reported in a financial statement for the period in which they are recognized. If this information is presented within a single continuous income statement, the presentation encompasses the following:

- Net income and its components
- Other comprehensive income and its components
- Total comprehensive income

In addition, the total of other comprehensive income for the reporting period must be stated in the balance sheet in a component of equity that is stated separately from the other equity line items.

EXAMPLE

Armadillo Ranch reports accumulated OCI within the equity section of its balance sheet as follows:

Equity:	
Contributed capital	$300,000
Retained capital	50,000
Accumulated other comprehensive income	20,000
Total equity	$370,000

Derivative Accounting

The essential accounting for a derivative instrument is outlined in the following bullet points:

- *Initial recognition.* When it is first acquired, recognize a derivative instrument in the balance sheet as an asset or liability at its fair value.
- *Subsequent recognition (hedging relationship).* Recognize all subsequent changes in the fair value of the derivative (known as *marked to market*). If the instrument has been paired with a hedged item, then recognize these fair value changes in other comprehensive income.
- *Subsequent recognition (ineffective portion).* Recognize all subsequent changes in the fair value of the derivative. If the instrument has been paired with a hedged item but the hedge is not effective, then recognize these fair value changes in earnings.

Hedge Accounting - General

The accounting for hedges involves matching a derivative instrument to a hedged item and then recognizing gains and losses from both items in the same period. A derivative is always measured at its fair value. If the instrument is effective for a period of time, this may mean that incremental changes in its fair value are continually being recorded in the accounting records.

The intent behind hedge accounting is to allow a farm to record changes in the value of a hedging relationship in other comprehensive income (except for fair value hedges), rather than in earnings. This is done in order to protect the core earnings of a farm from periodic variations in the value of its financial instruments before they have been liquidated. Once a financial instrument has been liquidated, any accumulated gains or losses stored in other comprehensive income are shifted into earnings.

When a farm uses a derivative as a hedge, it can elect to designate the derivative as belonging to one of the following three hedging classifications:

- *Fair value hedge*. The derivative is used to hedge the risk of changes in the fair value of an asset or liability, or of an unrecognized firm commitment. For example, a fair value hedge would apply to stored crops inventory.
- *Cash flow hedge*. The derivative is used to hedge variations in the cash flows associated with an asset or liability, or of a forecasted transaction. For example, a cash flow hedge would apply to growing crops, future crops, or livestock that is being raised or will be raised.
- *Foreign currency hedge*. The derivative is used to hedge variations in the foreign currency exposure associated with a net investment in a foreign operation, a forecasted transaction, an available-for-sale security, or an unrecognized firm commitment. This hedge probably does not apply to an agricultural operation, so we do not cover this option further.

If a derivative instrument is designated as belonging within one of these classifications, the gains or losses associated with the hedge are matched to any gains or losses incurred by the asset or liability with which the derivative is paired. However, the hedging relationship must first qualify for hedge accounting. To do so, the relationship must meet all of the following criteria:

- *Designation*. The hedging relationship must be designated as such at its inception. The documentation of the relationship must include the following:
  - The hedging relationship
  - The risk management objective and strategy, which includes identification of the hedging instrument and the hedged item, the nature of the risk being hedged, and the method used to determine hedge effectiveness and ineffectiveness.
  - If there is a fair value hedge of a firm commitment, a method for recognizing in earnings the asset or liability that represents the gain or loss on the hedged commitment.
  - If there is a cash flow hedge of a forecasted transaction, the period when the forecasted transaction will occur, the nature of the asset or liability involved, the number of items encompassed by the transaction, and the current price of the forecasted transaction.

- *Eligibility (hedged item).* Only certain types of assets and liabilities can qualify for special accounting as a hedging relationship.
- *Eligibility (hedging item).* Designate either all or a portion of the hedging instrument as such. Also, several derivative instruments can be jointly designated as the hedging instrument.
- *Effectiveness.* There is an expectation that the pairing will result in a highly effective hedge that offsets prospective changes in the cash flows or fair value associated with the hedged risk. A highly effective hedge is one in which the change in fair value or cash flows of the hedge falls between 80% and 125% of the opposing change in the fair value or cash flows of the financial instrument that is being hedged. Over the life of a hedging relationship, the effectiveness of the pairing must be examined at least quarterly. A prospective analysis should also be made to estimate whether the relationship will be highly effective in future periods, typically using a probability-weighted analysis of changes in fair value or cash flows. If the relationship is no longer highly effective through the date of this assessment, then the pairing no longer qualifies for hedge accounting.

If a hedging relationship is not fully documented or is never documented at all, then all subsequent changes in fair value associated with these instruments must be immediately recorded as gains or losses in earnings.

Hedge Accounting – Fair Value Hedges

The fair value of an asset or liability could change, which may affect the profits of a farm. A fair value hedge is designed to hedge against this exposure to changes in fair value that are caused by a specific risk. It is possible to only hedge the risks associated with a portion of an asset or liability, as long as the effectiveness of the related hedge can be measured.

When a hedging relationship has been established for a fair value hedge, continually re-measure the fair value of the hedge and the item with which it is paired. The accounting for this re-measurement is as follows:

- *Hedging item.* Record a gain or loss in earnings for the change in fair value of the hedging instrument.
- *Hedged item.* Record a gain or loss in earnings for the change in fair value of the hedged item that can be attributed to the risk for which the hedge pairing was established. This also means that the carrying amount of the hedged item must be adjusted to reflect its change in fair value.

If the hedging relationship is fully effective, either the gain on the hedging instrument will exactly offset the loss on the hedged item that is associated with the hedged risk, or vice versa. The net result of a fully effective hedge is no change in earnings. If there is a net gain or loss appearing in earnings, it is due to hedge ineffectiveness, where the hedging relationship does not perfectly offset fair value changes in the hedged item.

Fair value hedge accounting should be terminated at once if any of the following situations arise:

- The hedging arrangement is no longer effective
- The hedging instrument expires or is sold or terminated
- The farm revokes the hedging designation

Hedge Accounting – Cash Flow Hedges

There could be variations in the cash flows associated with an asset or liability or a forecasted transaction, which may affect the profits of a farm. A cash flow hedge is designed to hedge against this exposure to changes in cash flows that are caused by a specific risk. It is possible to only hedge the risks associated with a portion of an asset, liability, or forecasted transaction, as long as the effectiveness of the related hedge can be measured. The accounting for a cash flow hedge is as follows:

- *Hedging item.* Recognize the effective portion of any gain or loss in other comprehensive income, and recognize the ineffective portion of any gain or loss in earnings.
- *Hedged item.* Initially recognize the effective portion of any gain or loss in other comprehensive income. Reclassify these gains or losses into earnings when the forecasted transaction affects earnings.

A key issue with cash flow hedges is when to recognize gains or losses in earnings when the hedging transaction relates to a forecasted transaction. These gains or losses should be reclassified from other comprehensive income to earnings when the hedged transaction affects earnings.

Cash flow hedge accounting should be terminated at once if any of the following situations arises:

- The hedging arrangement is no longer effective
- The hedging instrument expires or is terminated
- The farm revokes the hedging designation

If it is probable that the hedged forecasted transaction will not occur within the originally-stated time period or within two months after this period, shift the derivative's gain or loss from accumulated other comprehensive income to earnings.

Summary

The accounting for derivatives and hedges is among the most complex in all of accounting, especially for outlier situations where the circumstances must be closely examined to ensure that the proper accounting rules are followed. In many instances, and especially when the farm accountant is dealing with a new transaction, it can make sense to consult with the farm's auditors regarding the proper accounting to use.

The payoff for this high level of accounting complexity is a delay in the recognition of gains or losses in earnings. If the farm manager is not concerned about more immediate recognition, or if the gains or losses are minor, it may make sense to ignore the multitude of compliance issues associated with hedge accounting. Instead, simply create hedges as needed and record gains or losses on hedges at once, without worrying about the proper documentation of each hedging relationship and having to repeatedly measure hedge effectiveness.

Chapter 14
Cooperative Accounting

Introduction

An agricultural cooperative is a business association into which farmers pool their resources. By doing so, farmers can increase their revenues, reduce costs or share risks, depending on the type of cooperative.

There are two types of farmers that interact with a cooperative. A *patron* is any person or other entity with which a cooperative does business on a cooperative basis. A *member* is an owner-patron, who can vote at its corporate meetings.

The following are common types of cooperatives:

- *Supply and service cooperatives.* These entities produce or buy goods and materials for their members. The prices charged are typically at market rates, but cooperatives may distribute patronage refunds to their members, thereby reducing member costs.
- *Marketing cooperatives.* These entities provide sales outlets for the products supplied to them by their members and patrons.
- *Federated cooperatives.* These are associations of cooperatives within a region.

A cooperative has the following characteristics:

- Its earnings are usually distributed to its patrons based on their proportional patronage of the cooperative, though some profits may be retained in the organization. In essence, all amounts received in excess of costs are returned to patrons.
- Cooperative members control the organization due to their roles as patrons; there are no equity investors.
- Membership in the cooperative is limited to patrons.
- At least half of the cooperative's business is performed on a patronage basis.
- There is a limited return paid out on capital investment.
- Earnings allocated back to patrons are treated as a tax deduction; earnings not allocated are taxed at the corporate income tax rate.

In this chapter, we describe the accounting by a cooperative and its patrons for certain types of transactions.

Cooperative Accounting

We begin with the accounting for transactions between a cooperative and its patrons from the perspective of the cooperative, as noted in the following sub-sections.

Inventory Accounting

The board of directors of a marketing cooperative may assign amounts approximating estimated market prices to unprocessed products that have been received from patrons. If so, these assigned amounts are considered to be the cost of the received products, and so can be charged to the cost of goods sold. If the board does not take this approach, the cooperative must instead account for inventories at net realizable value. *Net realizable value* is the estimated selling price of something in the ordinary course of business, with deductions for costs of completion, disposal, and transport.

EXAMPLE

The High Plains Cooperative experiences sales of $200,000 in the current year. The controller of High Plains is experimenting with different ways to record inventory. His choices are to do so at the lower of cost or market, or at the net realizable value of the inventory. He begins with the lower of cost or market approach, and arrives at the following cost summary for the year:

Lower of Cost or Market Calculation

Beginning inventory	$35,000
Assigned value of patrons' raw product received	145,000
Ending inventory	-39,000
Other costs and expenses	42,000
Total costs and expenses	$183,000

He then calculates expenses using net realizable value for the inventory, which alters the amounts of the beginning and ending inventory valuations. The assigned value of patrons' raw product received remains the same. The result appears in the following cost summary:

Net Realizable Value Calculation

Beginning inventory	$38,000
Assigned value of patrons' raw product received	145,000
Ending inventory	-45,500
Other costs and expenses	42,000
Total costs and expenses	$179,500

The impact of these two methods on the net earnings of High Plains is shown side-by-side in the following table. In the table, a small amount of income is stated for transactions that are not exempt from income taxation.

Net Earnings under differing Inventory Costing Assumptions

	Lower of Cost or Market Approach	Net Realizable Value Approach
Sales	$200,000	$200,000
Total costs and expenses	183,000	179,500
Earnings before income taxes	17,000	20,500
Income taxes	3,000	3,000
Net earnings	$14,000	$17,500

The controller then prepares a sample statement of amounts due to patrons, based on these two variations in calculating inventory costs. The results appear in the next table.

Statements of Amounts Due to Patrons

	Lower of Cost or Market Approach	Net Realizable Value Approach
Amounts due patrons at beginning of year	$8,500	$11,500
Net earnings	14,000	17,500
Assigned value of patrons' raw product received	145,000	145,000
Less: Amounts paid to patrons, retains, and non-patronage earnings	-157,000	-157,000
Amounts due patrons at end of year	$10,500	$17,000

The valuation methods used are different, so the beginning and ending inventory balances, as well as the amounts due patrons at the beginning and end of the year, will be different. In the following table, we quantify the difference between the two inventory valuation methods, which matches the difference between the amounts due to patrons at the end of the year under the two methods. In essence, a higher inventory valuation translates into a larger amount due to patrons at the end of the year.

Reconciliation of Statements of Amounts Due to Patrons

Ending inventory valuations based on:	
Lower of cost or market	$39,000
Net realizable value	45,500
Difference	-$6,500
Amounts due patrons at end of year (lower of cost or market basis)	$10,500
Amounts due patrons at end of year (net realizable value basis)	17,000
Difference	-$6,500

Earnings Allocations

In order to equitably allocate earnings to patrons, a cooperative may account for revenues and expenses by function, such as doing so separately for the supply department and the marketing department. When expenses are common to several functions, they are allocated to the functions on an equitable basis, using a consistently-applied methodology. When one function earns a profit and another function incurs a loss, there are several ways in which a cooperative could deal with the situation. For example:

- Charge the loss to unallocated retained capital.
- Offset the profits and losses against each other, and then allocate the remaining profit to the patrons of the profitable departments.
- Recover the loss from the patrons of the losing function.
- Subtract the loss from net non-patronage income. However, this may not eliminate the income tax liability associated with the non-patronage income.

Loss Allocations

A cooperative may incur a loss. There are a number of ways in which a cooperative can allocate this loss, including the following:

- Allocate the loss to patrons based on their patronage, where the allocation is offset against their equity or future allocations.
- Allocate the loss to patrons based on their equity; this can be inequitable when a high-equity patron is experiencing reduced patronage.
- Offset the loss against the amounts that will be available for patronage allocation in later years.
- Charge the loss to unallocated retained capital; this approach is most valid when the loss is attributable to the cooperative's business with non-patrons.

Liabilities

A marketing cooperative may assign amounts approximating market prices to patrons for their unprocessed products. If so, the assigned amounts are recognized as a liability for amounts due to patrons.

A cooperative typically pays its patrons on a short-term basis for the assigned amounts owed to them. Any excess of the cooperative's revenues over the assigned amounts and operating costs of the business is later paid or allocated to the patrons. The intervals at which these payments are made is contained within the operating rules of the cooperative, and could range from as little as once a week to longer than once a year.

Marketing cooperatives may deduct retains from the proceeds that are payable to patrons. These amounts are instead placed in the capital accounts of the patrons. These retained funds are essentially a form of financing for the cooperative. Retains are usually paid out over a number of subsequent years, and so can be considered liabilities of the cooperative. As such, they should be classified as liabilities on the balance sheet of a cooperative.

Presentation Issues

The revenues earned by a cooperative either come from patrons or non-patrons. The earnings from each of these groups should be reported on separate line items in the income statement. Non-patron earnings can include all of the following:

- Income earned on sales or purchases involving non-patrons
- Rental income related to non-patrons
- Income from investments in securities

The equity section of a cooperative's balance sheet includes investments in the entity by members and non-members, as well as from patronage allocations. When retained patron allocations and retains do not have a payment maturity date and are subordinated to all of a cooperative's debt instruments, they are to be presented on the balance sheet as equity. As equity, the cooperative must disclose all relevant information about these items, including the face value, dividend rate, negotiability, subordination agreements, payment plans, and so forth.

The board of directors of the cooperative will eventually decide when to pay allocated equities. The amounts to be paid are classified as current liabilities when the board has formally decided to pay them.

A cooperative may also accumulate unallocated retained capital; these earnings come from after-tax earnings on non-patronage business. These earnings are presented as retained capital in the equity section of the balance sheet.

Patron Accounting

A patron interacts with a cooperative in several ways, which triggers a number of transactions that must be properly recorded in the accounting records. We deal with them in the following sub-sections.

Deliveries Made to Marketing Cooperatives

When a patron delivers products to a marketing cooperative and there are indications that the expected net proceeds will be lower than cost, the patron should record the unbilled receivable at its estimated net realizable value. Once the amount of the proceeds is reasonably determinable, the variance from the amount recorded as an unbilled receivable can be recognized.

Inventory Delivered to a Marketing Cooperative

A patron may deliver products to a cooperative, with title to the product not passing to the cooperative. In addition, the identity of the product as being owned by the patron is maintained by the cooperative. Further, the price to be paid to the patron is based on the sale of the product, which has not yet occurred. Under these circumstances, the farm accountant must continue to record the inventory in the farm's accounting records. Only when the product has been sold by the cooperative can the accountant recognize a sale.

Advances from a Marketing Cooperative

A patron may receive an advance from a cooperative. This is a payment in advance of the final settlement, so it should be treated as a reduction of the patron's unbilled receivable. An advance is not to be recognized as a sale.

Accrual of Patronage Refunds

A patron can recognize patronage refunds in either of the following situations:

- Upon notification of payment by the distributing agricultural cooperative; or
- When all of the following are probable:
    - A patronage refund that applies to the period will be declared
    - Future events that will confirm receipt of the refund are expected to occur
    - The amount of the refund can be reasonably estimated
    - The accrual can be consistently made over time

The accrual is to be based on the latest available reliable information. For example, if a notification of payment by the distributing cooperative is superseded by a replacement notification, the second notification is used as the basis for the accrual.

If a patronage refund has already been accrued, the patron should adjust it when notified of the actual allocation amount by the cooperative.

Summary

Depending on the circumstances, a farm may conduct the bulk of its business with one or more local cooperatives. If so, the farm accountant should create procedures for handling a small number of recurring transactions. The result can be an extremely efficient accounting operation, since the accountant only needs to track the interactions of the farm with a small number of customers and suppliers.

In this chapter, we only dealt with the ongoing transactions between a cooperative and its patrons. In addition, members must account for their investments in a cooperative, including the initial investment, subsequent changes, and impairments of the investment. Since this type of investment is considered to be long-term, we have included the discussion in the Non-Current Farm Assets chapter.

Chapter 15
Revenue Recognition

Introduction

Revenue recognition involves fulfilling the accounting-mandated circumstances under which revenue can be recognized. A farm can recognize revenue when all activities related to a sale have been completed, and when an exchange had taken place between the farm and a buyer (such as selling crops for cash). The transactions that most clearly fulfill these requirements are the outright sale of products, such as crops, livestock, or livestock products. These situations likely address the bulk of all farm sales. In addition, we note several circumstances in the following sections that can also trigger the recognition of revenue.

Effects of Inventory Valuation using Net Realizable Value

A farm can recognize revenue when the production process is complete but products have not yet been sold. This situation arises when certain inventory items that are ready for sale are valued at their net realizable value, which is essentially the selling price minus delivery costs. The specific accounting for this situation is dealt with in the Inventory Accounting chapter. The recognition of this additional revenue is based on the view that most farm products are commodities that are actively traded. Thus, revenue recognition in this situation can only occur when there is little doubt about the ability to sell the products, nor the prices at which they can be sold.

Government Programs

The government may sponsor an income replacement or subsidy program. These programs are designed to increase farm earnings related to their production of certain commodities. These programs can include one or more of the following:

- Subsidy payments that are intended to increase farm earnings when commodities are suffering from low market prices.
- Disaster payments made to farms when disasters interfere with crop yields.
- Payments made to reimburse farms when they withhold land from production.
- Indemnities for other types of losses.

All of these payments are revenue to the recipient. The farm accountant should recognize these payments as revenue when the amount of the payment and the right to receive it can be reasonably determined.

Sales to Cooperatives

When a patron delivers product to a cooperative, the patron can record a sale at the point of delivery. However, the following conditions must be present in order to do so:

- Title has transferred to the cooperative
- A price is available based on current market transactions or the cooperative has established an assigned amount

If the patron sees a reasonable indication that the proceeds paid out by the cooperative will be less than the market price or the assigned amount, then the patron shall record the sale at the lower amount.

A different treatment is used by the patron when title has passed to the cooperative, but there is no stable price at which to record the sale. In this case, the patron should instead record the sale at the recorded amount of the inventory, with an offsetting unbilled account receivable. If there is a reasonable indication that the proceeds paid out by the cooperative will be less than the receivable, then the patron shall record the sale at the lower amount.

Commodity Credit Corporation Loans

The federal government runs the Commodity Credit Corporation (CCC), which is an agency of the U.S. Department of Agriculture. A farmer can offer crops to the CCC as collateral on a loan. The loan and accrued interest are then classified as current liabilities of the farm, since they are to be paid off within one year.

If the farm manager elects to do so, he can repay the loan by forfeiting the crop to the CCC. When this is the case, the act of forfeiting the crops is essentially a sale, with the amount of the original loan now becoming income for the farmer. In this situation, revenue recognition occurs when title to the crop passes to the CCC.

An additional reason for forfeiting a crop is that the farm pays no interest on the loan. Conversely, if the farm sells its produce elsewhere and then repays the loan in cash, the farm must pay interest on the loan.

EXAMPLE

The manager of Hillside Farm obtains a $200,000 from the Commodity Credit Corporation, for which the collateral is an amount of the farm's wheat crop equal to the loan. The initial journal entry is:

	Debit	Credit
Cash [asset account]	200,000	
Short-term loans [liability account]		200,000

After five months, the farm manager decides to repay the loan by forfeiting the crop. Doing so converts the loan into revenue, which is recorded with the following entry:

	Debit	Credit
Short-term loans [liability account]	200,000	
Sales – crops [revenue account]		200,000

Before a farm manager decides to take this approach, he should be aware of the IRS rules related to converting CCC loans to revenue, as stated in the following IRS pronouncement:

> Normally, you do not report loans you receive as income, and you report income from a crop for the year you sell it. However, if you pledge part or all of your production to secure a CCC loan, you can choose to treat the loan as if it were a sale of the crop and report the loan proceeds as income for the year you receive them. You do not need approval from the IRS to adopt this method of reporting CCC loans, even though you may have reported those received in earlier years as taxable income for the year you sold the crop. **Once you report a CCC loan as income for the year received, you must report all CCC loans in that year and later years in the same way, unless you get approval from the IRS to change to a different method.**

Forward Contracts

There may be a situation in which a farmer agrees in advance to sell his crops or livestock under the terms of a forward contract. In this arrangement, the sale has already occurred but the production process is not yet complete, so no revenue can be recognized until the production process is complete.

Summary

We have noted several circumstances in this chapter that can lead to (or delay) the recognition of revenue. Each one is tied to the specific accounting practices of the individual farm. Thus, loans are only convertible into revenue when the arrangement is with the CCC. Similarly, revenue will not be recognized when inventory is held for sale unless the inventory is valued at its net realizable value. Consequently, the farm accountant needs to be aware of which revenue recognition rules apply; also, the farm manager should be aware of these issues, since certain management decisions taken can impact the amount and timing of revenue recognition.

Chapter 16
Financial Statement Preparation

Introduction

The concept of closing the books refers to summarizing the information in the accounting records into the financial statements at the end of a reporting period. Many steps are required to do so. In this chapter, we give an overview of closing journal entries and the most prevalent closing activities that a farm is likely to need.

The sections in this chapter do not necessarily represent the exact sequence of activities that one should follow when closing the books; the sequence should be based on the unique processes of a farm and the availability of people to work on closing tasks.

Related Podcast Episodes: Episodes 16 through 25 and 160 of the Accounting Best Practices Podcast discuss closing the books. They are available at: **accounting-tools.com/podcasts** or **iTunes**

The Accruals Concept

An accrual is a journal entry that is used to recognize revenues and expenses that have been earned or consumed, respectively, and for which the related source documents have not yet been received or generated. Accruals are needed to ensure that all revenue and expense elements are recognized within the correct reporting period, irrespective of the timing of related cash flows. Without accruals, the amount of revenue, expense, and profit or loss in a period will not necessarily reflect the actual level of economic activity within a farm. Accruals are a key part of the closing process used to create financial statements under the accrual basis of accounting; without accruals, financial statements would be considerably less accurate.

It is most efficient to initially record most accruals as reversing entries. This is a useful feature when a farm is expecting to issue an invoice for product sold or receive an invoice from a supplier in the following period. For example, a farm accountant may know that a supplier invoice for $20,000 will arrive a few days after the end of a month, but he wants to close the books as soon as possible. Accordingly, he records a $20,000 reversing entry to recognize the expense in the current month. In the next month, the accrual reverses, creating a negative $20,000 expense that is offset by the arrival and recordation of the supplier invoice.

Examples of accruals that a farm might record are:

- *Expense accrual for interest.* A local lender issues a loan to a farm and sends the borrower an invoice each month, detailing the amount of interest owed. The borrower can record the interest expense in advance of invoice receipt by recording accrued interest.
- *Expense accrual for wages.* A farm pays its employees once a month for the hours they have worked through the 26th day of the month. The farm accountant can accrue all additional wages earned from the 27th through the last day of the month, to ensure that the full amount of the wage expense is recognized.
- *Sales accrual.* A farm sells produce to a major government agency, which it is contractually limited to billing on a quarterly basis. In the meantime, the farm can accrue revenue for the amount of agricultural produce provided to date, even though the charges have not yet been billed.

Adjusting Entries

Adjusting entries are journal entries that are used at the end of an accounting period to adjust the balances in various general ledger accounts to more closely align the reported results and financial position of a business to meet the requirements of an accounting framework, such as Generally Accepted Accounting Principles (GAAP).

An adjusting entry can be used for any type of accounting transaction; here are some of the more common ones:

- To record depreciation for the period
- To record an allowance for doubtful accounts
- To record accrued revenue
- To record accrued expenses
- To record previously paid but unused expenditures as prepaid expenses
- To adjust cash balances for any reconciling items noted in the bank reconciliation

Adjusting entries are most commonly of three types, which are:

- *Accruals.* To record a revenue or expense that has not yet been recorded through a standard accounting transaction.
- *Deferrals.* To defer a revenue or expense that has occurred, but which has not yet been earned or used.
- *Estimates.* To estimate the amount of a reserve, such as the allowance for doubtful accounts.

When a journal entry is recorded for an accrual, deferral, or estimate, it usually impacts an asset or liability account. For example, if an expense is accrued, this also increases a liability account. Or, if revenue recognition is deferred to a later period, this also increases a liability account. Thus, adjusting entries impact the balance sheet, not just the income statement.

Reversing Entries

When a journal entry is created, it may be to record revenue or an expense other than through a more traditional method, such as issuing an invoice to a customer or recording an invoice from a supplier. In these situations, the journal entry is only meant to be a stopgap measure, with the traditional recordation method still being used at a later date. This means that the farm accountant has to eventually create a journal entry that is the *opposite* of the original entry, thereby cancelling out the original entry. The concept is best explained with an example.

EXAMPLE

The accountant for Lincoln Farms has not yet received an invoice from a feed supplier by the time he closes the books for the month of May. He expects that the invoice will be for $2,000, so he records the following accrual entry for the invoice:

	Debit	Credit
Purchased feed [expense account]	2,000	
Accrued expenses [liability account]		2,000

This entry creates an additional expense of $2,000 for the month of May.

The accountant knows that the invoice will arrive in June and will be recorded upon receipt. Therefore, he creates a reversing entry for the original accrual in early June that cancels out the original entry. The entry is:

	Debit	Credit
Accrued expenses [liability account]	2,000	
Purchased feed [expense]		2,000

The invoice then arrives, and is recorded in the normal manner through the accounts payable module in Lincoln's accounting software. This creates an expense during the month of June of $20,000. Thus, the net effect in June is:

June reversing entry	-$20,000
Supplier invoice	+20,000
Net effect in June	$0

Thus, the accrual entry shifts recognition of the expense from June to May.

Any accounting software package contains an option for automatically creating a reversing journal entry when a journal entry is initially set up. Always use this feature when a reversing entry will be needed. By doing so, the farm accountant can avoid the risk of forgetting to manually create the reversing entry, and also avoid the risk of creating an incorrect entry.

Tip: There will be situations where there is no need to reverse a journal entry for a few months. If so, consider using an automated reversing entry in the *next* month, and creating a replacement journal entry in each successive month. While this approach may appear time-consuming, it ensures that the original entry is *always* flushed from the books, thereby avoiding the risk of carrying a journal entry past the date when it should have been eliminated.

Common Adjusting Entries

This section contains a discussion of the journal entries that are most likely to be needed to close the books, along with an example of the accounts most likely to be used in the entries.

Accrued Expenses

If there are supplier invoices that the accountant is aware of but has not yet received, estimate the amount of the expense and accrue it with a journal entry. There are any number of expense accounts to which such transactions might be charged; in the following sample entry, we assume that the expense relates to a supplier invoice for utilities that has not yet arrived.

	Debit	Credit
Utilities expense [expense account]	xxx	
Accrued expenses [liability account]		xxx

This is likely to be the most frequent of the adjusting entries, as there may be a number of supplier invoices that do not arrive by the time the books are closed.

Accrued Revenue

If a farm has delivered livestock or crops but has not yet issued an invoice to the customer, the farm accountant can accrue the associated amount of revenue. This entry is a credit to a revenue account, with an offsetting entry to an accrued accounts receivable account. Do not record this accrual in the standard trade accounts receivable account, since that account should be reserved for actual billings to customers. A sample of the accrued revenue entry is:

	Debit	Credit
Accounts receivable – accrued [asset account]	xxx	
Sales [revenue account]		xxx

Allowance for Doubtful Accounts

If a farm sells livestock or crops on credit, it is possible that a portion of the resulting accounts receivable will eventually become bad debts. If so, update the allowance for doubtful accounts each month. This account is a contra asset account that offsets the balance in the accounts receivable account. Set the balance in this allowance to match the best estimate of how much of the month-end accounts receivable will eventually be written off as bad debts. A sample entry is:

	Debit	Credit
Bad debts expense [expense account]	xxx	
Allowance for doubtful accounts [contra asset account]		xxx

Prepaid Expenses

Occasionally, a significant payment is made in advance to a third party. This advance may be for something that will be charged to expense in a later period, or it may be a deposit that will be returned to the farm at a later date. These payments should initially be recorded as assets, usually in the prepaid expenses account. The entry for doing so is described in the Accounting Transactions chapter.

When the books are closed, a portion of these assets are charged to expense, depending upon the extent to which they have been consumed. The exact journal entry will vary, depending on the contents of the prepaid assets account. For example, if a full year of crop insurance was purchased in advance and then is charged to expense as part of the closing process at the rate of $1/12^{th}$ per month, the journal entry would be:

	Debit	Credit
Insurance expense [expense account]	xxx	
Prepaid expenses [asset account]		xxx

Unpaid Taxes

A farm has a liability for any number of taxes, including property taxes, payroll taxes, and income taxes. These taxes are due on certain dates, as mandated by the applicable governments. If the payment date happens to fall on a day later than the end of a reporting period, then the farm has an unpaid tax liability. In some cases, such as with property taxes, an invoice is received for the amount due, which is processed through the accounts payable system.

In other cases, such as income taxes, there is no invoice – so the farm accountant needs to record an entry for unpaid taxes. For example, the following journal entry is designed to accrue for the unpaid income taxes:

	Debit	Credit
Income tax expense [expense account]	xxx	
Accrued expenses [liability account]		xxx

Create Customer Invoices

Part of the closing process may include the issuance of month-end invoices to customers. A farm may have few invoices, if any – and certainly not if it is paid in cash by its customers. If it is delivering livestock or crops to a cooperative, then verify that the accounting records contain evidence of each delivery that translates into revenue.

If some revenues are considered to not yet be billable, but to have been fully earned by the farm, accrue the revenue with a journal entry.

The accounting software should have an accounts receivable module that is used to enter customer invoices. This module automatically populates the accounts receivable account in the general ledger when invoices are created. Thus, at month-end, one can print the aged accounts receivable report and have the grand total on it match the ending balance in the accounts receivable general ledger account. This means that there are no reconciling items between the aged accounts receivable report and the general ledger account.

If there is a difference between the two numbers, it is almost certainly caused by the use of a journal entry that debited or credited the accounts receivable account. The farm accountant should *never* create such a journal entry, because there is so much detail in the accounts receivable account that it is very time-consuming to wade through it to ascertain the source of the variance.

The primary transaction that the farm accountant will be tempted to record in the accounts receivable account is accrued revenue. Instead, create a current asset account called "Accrued Revenue Receivable" and enter the accruals in that account. By doing so, normal accounts receivable transactions are segregated from special month-end accrual transactions.

Reconcile the Bank Statement

Closing cash is all about the bank reconciliation, because it matches the amount of cash recorded by the farm to what its bank has recorded. Once a bank reconciliation has been constructed, the accountant can have considerable confidence that the amount of cash appearing on the balance sheet is correct.

It is extremely important to complete a bank reconciliation for every account that contains a significant amount of cash. This is needed to obtain an understanding of the types and timing of cash flows and the unrecorded transactions that can arise, as well as to ensure that the farm's cash balance information is correct.

A likely outcome of the reconciliation process will be several adjustments to a farm's recorded cash balance. It is unlikely that the farm's ending cash balance and the bank's ending cash balance will be identical, since there are probably multiple payments and deposits in transit at all times, as well as bank service fees, penalties, and not sufficient funds deposits that the farm has not yet recorded.

The essential process flow for a bank reconciliation is to start with the bank's ending cash balance (known as the *bank balance*), add to it any deposits in transit from the farm to the bank, subtract any checks that have not yet cleared the bank, and either add or deduct any other reconciling items. Then find the farm's ending cash balance and deduct from it any bank service fees, not sufficient funds (NSF) checks and penalties, and add to it any interest earned. At the end of this process, the adjusted bank balance should equal the farm's ending adjusted cash balance.

The following bank reconciliation procedure assumes that the bank reconciliation is being created in an accounting software package, which makes the reconciliation process easier:

1. Enter the bank reconciliation software module. A listing of uncleared checks and uncleared deposits will appear.
2. Check off in the bank reconciliation module all checks that are listed on the bank statement as having cleared the bank.
3. Check off in the bank reconciliation module all deposits that are listed on the bank statement as having cleared the bank.
4. Enter as expenses all bank charges appearing on the bank statement, and which have not already been recorded in the company's records.
5. Enter the ending balance on the bank statement. If the book and bank balances match, then post all changes recorded in the bank reconciliation and close the module. If the balances do *not* match, then continue reviewing the bank reconciliation for additional reconciling items. Look for the following items:

   - Checks recorded in the bank records at a different amount from what is recorded in the farm's records.
   - Deposits recorded in the bank records at a different amount from what is recorded in the farm's records.
   - Checks recorded in the bank records that are not recorded at all in the farm's records.
   - Deposits recorded in the bank records that are not recorded at all in the farm's records.
   - Inbound wire transfers from which a processing fee has been extracted.

EXAMPLE

Sunlight Farm is closing its books for the month ended April 30. Sunlight's accountant must prepare a bank reconciliation based on the following issues:

1. The bank statement contains an ending bank balance of $320,000.
2. The bank statement contains a $200 check printing charge for new checks that the farm ordered.
3. The bank statement contains a $150 service charge for operating the bank account.
4. The bank rejected a deposit of $500 due to not sufficient funds, and charges the farm a $10 fee associated with the rejection.
5. The bank statement contains interest income of $30.
6. Sunlight issued $80,000 of checks that have not yet cleared the bank.
7. Sunlight deposited $25,000 of checks at month-end that were not deposited in time to appear on the bank statement.

The accountant creates the following reconciliation:

		Item #	Adjustment to Books
Bank balance	$320,000	1	
- Check printing charge	-200	2	Debit expense, credit cash
- Service charge	-150	3	Debit expense, credit cash
- NSF fee	-10	4	Debit expense, credit cash
- NSF deposit rejected	-500	4	Debit receivable, credit cash
+ Interest income	+30	5	Debit cash, credit interest income
- Uncleared checks	-80,000	6	None
+ Deposits in transit	+25,000	7	None
= Book balance	$264,170		

When the bank reconciliation process is complete, print a report through the accounting software that shows the bank and book balances, the identified differences between the two (most likely to be uncleared checks), and any remaining unreconciled difference. Retain a copy of this report for each month, since the auditors will want to see them as part of the year-end audit. The format of the report will vary by software package; a simplistic layout follows.

Sample Bank Reconciliation Statement

For the month ended March 31, 20x3		
Bank balance	$85,000	
Less: Checks outstanding	-22,500	See detail
Add: Deposits in transit	+10,000	See detail
+/- Other adjustments	0	
Book balance	$72,500	
Unreconciled difference	$0	

The standard approach to bank reconciliations is to complete them for all accounts shortly after the end of each month, since the reconciliations are derived from the bank statements that are issued after month-end.

It is even better to conduct a bank reconciliation every day based on the bank's month-to-date information, which should be accessible on the bank's web site. By completing a daily bank reconciliation, the accountant can spot and correct problems immediately.

Calculate Depreciation

Once all fixed assets have been recorded in the accounting records for the month, calculate the amount of depreciation. This is a significant issue when there is a large investment in fixed assets, but may be so insignificant in other situations that it is sufficient to only record depreciation at the end of the year. Depreciation is covered in the Fixed Assets and Depreciation chapter.

Close Accounts Payable

Accounts payable can be a significant bottleneck in the closing process. The reason is that some suppliers only issue invoices at the end of each month when they are closing *their* books, so the farm will not receive its invoices until several days into the next month. This circumstance usually arises either when a supplier ships something near the end of the month or when it is providing a continuing service. There are several choices for dealing with these items:

1. *Do nothing.* By waiting a few days, the invoices will arrive in the mail, and the accountant can record the invoices and close the books. The advantage of this approach is a high degree of precision and perfect supporting evidence for all expenses. It is probably the best approach at year-end, if the farm manager plans to have the financial statements audited. The downside is that it can significantly delay the issuance of financial statements.
2. *Accrue continuing service items.* As just noted, suppliers providing continuing services are more likely to issue invoices at month-end. When services are being provided on a continuing basis, one can easily estimate what the expense should be, based on prior invoices. Thus, it is not difficult to create

reversing journal entries for these items at the end of the month. It is likely that these accruals will vary somewhat from the amounts on the actual invoices, but the differences should be immaterial.

3. *Accrue based on purchase orders.* As just noted, suppliers issue invoices at month-end when they ship goods near that date. If the farm is using purchase orders to order these items, the supplier is supposed to issue an invoice containing the same price stated on the purchase order. Therefore, if an item is received but there is no accompanying invoice, use the purchase order to create a reversing journal entry that accrues the expense associated with the received item.

In short, we strongly recommend using accruals to record expenses for supplier invoices that have not yet arrived. The sole exception is the end of the year, when the auditors may expect a greater degree of precision and supporting evidence, and so will expect the accountant to wait for actual invoices to arrive before closing the books.

The accounting software should have an accounts payable module that is used to enter supplier invoices. This module automatically populates the accounts payable account in the general ledger with transactions. Thus, at the end of the month, one can print the aged accounts payable report and have the grand total on that report match the ending balance in the accounts payable general ledger account; there are no reconciling items between the aged accounts payable report and the general ledger.

If there is a difference between the two numbers, it is almost certainly caused by the use of a journal entry that debited or credited the accounts payable account. The accountant should *never* create such a journal entry, because there is so much detail in the accounts payable account that it is very time-consuming to wade through it to ascertain the source of the variance.

The one transaction that the accountant will be tempted to record in the accounts payable account is the accrued expense. Instead, create a current liability account in the general ledger called "Accrued Expenses" and enter the accruals in that account. By doing so, the accountant is properly segregating normal accounts payable transactions from special month-end accrual transactions.

This differentiation is not a minor one. Accrual transactions require more maintenance than standard accounts payable transactions, because they may linger through multiple accounting periods, and the accountant needs to monitor them to know when to eliminate them from the general ledger. This problem can be addressed with reversing journal entries, but some accruals may not be designated as reversing entries, which calls for long-term tracking. If the accountant were to lump accrued expenses into the accounts payable account, it would be very difficult to continually monitor the outstanding accruals.

In summary, restrict the accounts payable account to standard payables transactions, which makes it extremely easy to reconcile at month-end. Any transactions related to accounts payable but which are entered via journal entries should be recorded in a separate account.

Review Journal Entries

It is entirely possible that some journal entries were made incorrectly, in duplicate, or not at all. Print the list of standard journal entries and compare it to the actual entries made in the general ledger, just to ensure that they were entered in the general ledger correctly. Another test is to have someone review the detailed calculations supporting each journal entry, and trace them through to the actual entries in the general ledger. This second approach takes more time, but is useful for ensuring that all necessary journal entries have been made correctly.

If there is an interest in closing the books quickly, the latter approach could interfere with the speed of the close; if so, authorize this detailed review at a later date, when someone can conduct the review under less time pressure. However, any errors found can only be corrected in the *following* accounting period, since the financial statements will already have been issued.

Reconcile Accounts

It is important to examine the contents of the balance sheet accounts to verify that the recorded assets and liabilities are supposed to be there. It is quite possible that some items are still listed in an account that should have been flushed out a long time ago, which can be quite embarrassing if they are still on record when the auditors review the farm's books at the end of the year. Here are several situations that a proper account reconciliation would have caught:

- *Prepaid assets.* A farm pays $5,000 to an insurance company as an advance on its regular monthly medical insurance and records the payment as a prepaid asset. The asset lingers on the books until year-end, when the auditors inquire about it, and the full amount is then charged to expense.
- *Depreciation.* A farm accountant calculates the depreciation on several hundred assets with an electronic spreadsheet, which unfortunately does not track when to stop depreciating assets. A year-end review finds that the farm charged $18,000 of excess depreciation to expense.
- *Accumulated depreciation.* A farm has been disposing of its assets for years, but has never bothered to eliminate the associated accumulated depreciation from its balance sheet. Doing so reduces both the fixed asset and accumulated depreciation accounts by 50%.
- *Accounts payable.* A farm does not compare its accounts payable detail report to the general ledger account balance, which is $8,000 lower than the detail. The auditors spot the error and require a correcting entry at year-end, so that the account balance matches the detail report.

These issues and many more are common problems encountered at year-end. To prevent the extensive error corrections caused by these problems, conduct account reconciliations every month for the larger accounts, and occasionally review the detail for the smaller accounts, too. The following are some of the account reconciliations to conduct, as well as the specific issues to look for:

Sample Account Reconciliation List

Account	Reconciliation Discussion
Cash	There can be a number of unrecorded checks, deposits, and bank fees that can only be spotted with a bank reconciliation. It is permissible to do a partial bank reconciliation a day or two before the close, but completely ignoring it is not a good idea.
Accounts receivable, trade	The accounts receivable detail report should match the account balance. If not, the accountant probably created a journal entry that should be eliminated from this account.
Accounts receivable, other	This account usually includes a large proportion of accounts receivable from employees, which are probably being deducted from their paychecks over time. This is a prime source of errors, since payroll deductions may not have been properly reflected in this account.
Accrued revenue	It is good practice to reverse all accrued revenue out of this account at the beginning of every period, so that the accountant is forced to create new accruals every month. Thus, if there is a residual balance in the account, it probably should not be there.
Prepaid assets	This account may contain a variety of assets that will be charged to expense in the short term, so it may require frequent reviews to ensure that items have been flushed out in a timely manner.
Fixed assets	It is quite likely that fixed assets will initially be recorded in the wrong fixed asset account, or that they are disposed of incorrectly. Reconcile the account to the fixed asset detail report at least once a quarter to spot and correct these issues.
Accumulated depreciation	The balance in this account may not match the fixed asset detail if the accountant has not removed the accumulated depreciation from the account upon the sale or disposal of an asset. This is not a critical issue, but still warrants occasional review.
Accounts payable, trade	The accounts payable detail report should match the account balance. If not, the accountant probably included a journal entry in the account, and should reverse that entry.
Accrued expenses	This account can include a large number of accruals for such expenses as wages, vacations, and benefits. It is good practice to reverse all of these expenses in the month following recordation. Thus, if there is a residual balance, there may be an excess accrual still on the books.
Notes payable	The balance in this account should exactly match the account balance of the lender, barring any exceptions for in-transit payments to the lender.

The number of accounts that can be reconciled makes it clear that this is one of the larger steps involved in closing the books. The accountant can skip selected reconciliations from time to time, but doing so presents the risk of an error creeping into the financial statements and not being spotted for quite a few months. Consequently, there is a significant risk of issuing inaccurate financial statements if some reconciliations are routinely avoided.

Close Subsidiary Ledgers

Depending on the type of accounting software used, it may be necessary to resolve any open issues in subsidiary ledgers (such as for receivables and payables), create a transaction to shift the totals in these balances to the general ledger (called *posting*), and then close the accounting periods within the subsidiary ledgers and open the next accounting period.

Other accounting software systems (typically those developed more recently) do not have subsidiary ledgers, or at least use ones that do not require posting, and so are essentially invisible from the perspective of closing the books. We assume that the farm accountant is using one of the newer systems, so we will not delve deeper into the details of subsidiary ledgers.

Review Financial Statements

Once all of the preceding steps have been completed, print the financial statements and review them for errors. There are several ways to do so, including:

- *Horizontal analysis.* Print reports that show the income statement, balance sheet, and statement of cash flows for the past twelve months on a rolling basis. Track across each line item to see if there are any unusual declines or spikes in comparison to the results of prior periods, and investigate those items. This is the best review technique.
- *Budget versus actual.* Print an income statement that shows budgeted versus actual results, and investigate any larger variances. This is a less effective review technique, because it assumes that the budget is realistic, and also because a budget is not usually available for the balance sheet or statement of cash flows.

There will almost always be problems with the first iteration of the financial statements. Expect to investigate and correct several items before issuing a satisfactory set of financials. To reduce the amount of time needed to review financial statement errors during the core closing period, consider doing so a few days prior to month-end; this may uncover a few errors, leaving a smaller number to investigate later on.

Accrue Tax Liabilities

Once the financial statements have been printed and the information in them has been finalized, there may be a need to accrue an income tax liability based on the amount of net profit. There are several issues to consider when creating this accrual, which are covered in the Income Taxes chapter. Once an income tax liability has been accrued, print the complete set of financial statements.

Close the Month

Once all transactions have been entered into the accounting system, close the month in the accounting software. This means prohibiting any further transactions in the general ledger in the old accounting period, as well as allowing the next accounting period to accept transactions. These steps are important, so that the accountant does not inadvertently enter transactions into the wrong accounting periods.

Closing the month usually involves setting a flag in the accounting software, which can be accomplished with a few keystrokes. When the flag is set, the software creates a group of closing entries. Closing entries are journal entries used to flush out all temporary accounts at the end of an accounting period and transfer their balances into permanent accounts. Doing so resets the temporary accounts to begin accumulating new transactions in the next accounting period. A *temporary account* is an account used to hold balances during an accounting period for revenue, expense, gain, and loss transactions. These accounts are flushed into the retained capital account at the end of an accounting period. All other accounts are called *permanent accounts*, and retain their balances on an ongoing basis.

The basic sequence of closing entries is:

1. Debit all revenue accounts and credit the income summary account, thereby clearing out the revenue accounts.
2. Credit all expense accounts and debit the income summary account, thereby clearing out all expense accounts.
3. Close the income summary account to the retained capital account. If there was a profit in the period, this entry is a debit to the income summary account and a credit to the retained capital account. If there was a loss in the period, this entry is a credit to the income summary account and a debit to the retained capital account.

The net result of these activities is to move the net profit or loss for the period into the retained capital account, which appears in the equity section of the balance sheet.

Since the income summary account is only a transitional account, it is also acceptable to close directly to the retained capital account and bypass the income summary account entirely.

EXAMPLE

The accountant for Long Ridge Farm is closing the books for the most recent accounting period. Long Ridge had $50,000 of revenues and $45,000 of expenses during the period. For simplicity, we assume that all of the expenses were recorded in a single account; in a normal environment, there might be dozens of expense accounts to clear out. The sequence of entries is:

1. Empty the revenue account by debiting it for $50,000, and transfer the balance to the income summary account with a credit. The entry is:

	Debit	Credit
Revenue	50,000	
Income summary		50,000

2. Empty the expense account by crediting it for $45,000, and transfer the balance to the income summary account with a debit. The entry is:

	Debit	Credit
Income summary	45,000	
Expenses		45,000

3. Empty the income summary account by debiting it for $5,000 and transfer the balance to the retained capital account with a credit. The entry is:

	Debit	Credit
Income summary	5,000	
Retained capital		5,000

These entries have emptied the revenue, expense, and income summary accounts and shifted the net profit for the period to the retained capital account.

Add Disclosures

If the farm is issuing financial statements to readers other than the farm manager, consider adding disclosures to the basic set of financial statements. There are many disclosures required under GAAP. It is especially important to include a complete set of disclosures if the financial statements are being audited. If so, the auditors will offer advice regarding which disclosures to include. Allocate a large amount of time to the proper construction and error-checking of disclosures, for they contain a number of references to the financial statements and subsets of financial information extracted from the statements, and this information could be wrong. Thus, every time a new iteration of the financial statements is created, the accountant should update the disclosures.

If financial statements are being issued solely to the farm manager, do not include any disclosures. By avoiding them, the accountant can cut a significant amount of time from the closing process. Further, the manager is already well aware of how the farm is run, and so presumably does not need the disclosures.

Examples of the more common disclosures appear in the Financial Statement Disclosures chapter.

Issue Financial Statements

The final core step in closing the books is to issue the financial statements. There are several ways to do this. If there is an interest in reducing the total time required for someone to receive the financial statements, convert the entire package to PDF documents and e-mail them to the recipients. Doing so eliminates the mail float that would otherwise be required. If a number of reports are being integrated into the financial statement package, this may require the purchase of a document scanner.

When issuing financial statements, always print a copy and store it in a binder. This gives ready access to the report during the next few days, when the farm manager is most likely to contact the accountant with questions about it.

Summary

This chapter has outlined a number of steps that are needed to close the books. The level of organization required to close the books in this manner might appear to be overkill. However, consider that one of the most visible work products of the accountant is the financial statements. If this person can establish a reputation for consistently issuing high-quality financial statements within a reasonable period of time, the farm manager may be more willing to accept advice from the accountant in other areas.

There are a number of techniques available that allow a farm to close its books and issue financial statements within just a few days. For a comprehensive discussion of these techniques, see the author's *Closing the Books* book.

Chapter 17
Financial Statement Disclosures

Introduction

When a farm issues financial statements to anyone outside of the business, it is customary to provide them with a complete set of financial statements – which includes a number of disclosures. The precise nature of these disclosures depends on the farm and the types of transactions in which it engages; this means it is impossible to provide a complete set of disclosures that can be attached to *any* farm financial statements. Instead, disclosures must be tailored to the specific situation. In this chapter, we note a number of disclosures that the farm accountant will likely need to append to the financial statements, including examples.

Disclosure of Accounting Policies

A description of all significant accounting policies of a farm must be included in the notes that accompany the financial statements. Even in cases where only one or a few of the financial statements are released, the farm accountant should still include in the accompanying notes those accounting policies that most directly pertain to the statements being released.

> **Tip:** If the farm has not changed its accounting policies since its last fiscal year, and the financial statements are both unaudited and being released for an interim period, it is acceptable to not include accounting policies in the accompanying disclosures.

The accounting policies that should be disclosed by a farm are those that materially affect its financial position, cash flows, or results of operations, and explain the appropriateness of those principles concerning revenue recognition and cost allocations to current and future periods.

GAAP specifically requires that disclosure be made if an accounting principle involves an unusual application of GAAP, a selection among several valid alternatives, or principles peculiar to the entity's industry (in this case, agriculture).

In the following sub-sections, we note a number of the accounting policies that might be appended to a farm's financial statements.

Basis of Accounting

The basis of accounting refers to the methodology under which revenues and expenses are recognized in the financial statements of a business. The disclosure may include any accounting used by the farm that is not in compliance with the underlying methodology. For example:

> The accounting policies used in the creation of the Farm's financial statements use accrual-basis accounting, conforming to generally accepted accounting principles (GAAP) except for the manner in which the Farm values its raised breeding livestock. GAAP requires that raised breeding livestock be valued at their cost minus accumulated depreciation. The Farm values its raised breeding livestock at their base value, which can exceed cost minus accumulated depreciation. The effect of this difference has not been determined.

Nature of Operations

This disclosure contains a brief description of the farm's operations, including the following:

- The organizational structure or form of the farm
- The number of acres being farmed or ranched, and whether they are owned or leased
- The types of crops or livestock being produced
- The number of head raised, produced, milked, and so forth
- The nature of any non-farm business activities

For example:

> The owners, David and Susan Merman, operate the Farm as a subchapter S corporation. The Farm is comprised of 1,000 acres of owned land and an additional 200 rented acres. The principle cash crops of the Farm are sugar beets, wheat, and corn. Oats and hay are also grown for feed. The Farm supports 400 feeder cattle and 200 feeder pigs.

Use of Estimates

Disclose the nature of any estimates used in the derivation of the financial statements. For example, estimates may be required to weigh livestock and estimate the contents of grain bins. A sample disclosure is:

> In preparing these financial statements, management has made estimates that affect the reported amounts of assets, liabilities, revenues and expenses. Actual results may differ from these estimates.

> The Farm estimates the quantities of its feed and crop inventory as part of its quarterly physical inventory counts. The inventory is estimated by measuring the volume of grain in storage bins. This differs from the measurement technique used when grain

is sold, which is by weight. Thus, the estimated quantities on hand may differ from the actual quantities.

Basis of Combination

If the presented financial statements are combined with those of one or more other entities, the names of all the entities are stated. Also note whether the personal assets of the owners are included in the financial statements – a particular consideration for farm reporting. For example:

> The combined financial statements of Shady Ridge Farms include the accounts of Shady Ridge and Shady Oil Leasing Proprietorship. David Gauss owns 100% of the outstanding stock of Shady Ridge, which holds title to all of the assets in these financial statements, with the exception of the drilling platforms that are owned by Shady Oil Leasing. Mr. Gauss also owns 100% of Shady Oil Leasing. All material intercompany transactions have been eliminated. These financial statements do not include any personal assets of Mr. Gauss.

Cash and Cash Equivalents

Define what is considered to be a cash equivalent in the financial statements. For example:

> For the purposes of reporting cash and cash equivalents, the Farm considers all cash amounts not subject to withdrawal restrictions, as well as all debt securities with maturities equal to or less than three months, to be cash equivalents.

Trade Accounts and Other Receivables

State any material accounts receivable, as well as any material notes receivable. Further, note the basis of accounting for receivables, as well as the policy for charging off uncollectible receivables. For example:

> The Farm presents in its balance sheet the amount of accounts and notes receivable that it expects to receive as of the balance sheet date. The stated amount is considered to be collectible based on the payment histories of the Farm's customers, trend projections, and credit information regarding the customers. An allowance for doubtful accounts contains the estimated amount of accounts and notes receivable that management does not expect to be collected, which is offset against the outstanding receivable balances. The allowance contained $14,000 and $11,000 for the years ended December 31, 20X3 and 20X2, respectively.

Basis of Inventory Valuation

Describe the methods used to derive valuations for the farm's inventory, including feed, crops, livestock, and livestock products. For example:

> The Farm values all inventory purchased for use at cost. Inventory raised for use is valued at the lower of its cost or the cost at which it could currently be purchased on the market. Inventory raised for sale is valued at its net realizable value.

Revenue Recognition

State the circumstances under which the farm recognizes revenue. For example:

> The Farm recognizes revenue at the point when it receives cash for the sale of its crops. It also recognizes revenue from government price support programs when the cash is received. Also, if the Farm forfeits its crop to the Commodity Credit Corporation (CCC) under a loan payment program, the Farm recognizes revenue when title to the crops passes to the CCC.

Income Taxes

Define deferred taxes and how they are included in the financial statements. Also note how the farm handles tax positions. For example:

> The financial statements include taxes currently due, as well as deferred taxes. Deferred taxes are recognized when there are differences between the basis of assets and liabilities for financial statement and income tax reporting purposes. Deferred tax assets and liabilities are the tax return results of these differences, which will be either taxable or deductible as the assets or liabilities are recovered or settled.

> When preparing tax returns, the Farm takes tax positions based on management's interpretation of tax law. The Farm periodically examines these positions and evaluates their status; this can result in revisions to estimated amounts owed, including interest and penalties. No amounts have been recorded as uncertain tax positions.

Commitments

State the types of contractual arrangements into which the farm enters on a regular basis. These arrangements could include, for example, sales contracts and purchase contracts. A sample disclosure is:

> The Farm regularly enters into pricing agreements and option contracts for the sale of its crops. As of the balance sheet date, any unsettled pricing agreements and option contracts for current-year commodities are used to value the current year's unsold crops. Any pricing agreements and option contracts for future crop years are stated in other comprehensive income.

Disclosure of Inventory

Present a breakdown in tabular format of the valuations of the different classifications of inventory. For example:

	December 31	
	20X3	20X2
Feed – Purchased	$1,000	3,500
Feed – Raised	3,800	7,200
Livestock – Raised for sale	109,200	112,400
Total inventory	$114,000	$123,100

Disclosure of Raised Dairy and Breeding Livestock

The financial statements should include a summary of the classifications used by a farm to track its raised breeding livestock, including the number of animals and their recorded values. For example:

The Farm uses the full cost absorption method to value its breeding livestock. The cost of each classification of livestock, along with the number of animals, appears in the following table.

	Number of Animals	Cost per Head	Total Cost
Sows	192	$310	$59,520
Gilts	46	120	5,520
Boars	14	420	5,880
			$70,920

Disclosure of Fixed Assets

The financial statements should disclose the following information about a farm's fixed assets:

- *Accumulated depreciation.* The balances in each of the major classes of fixed assets as of the end of the reporting period.
- *Asset aggregation.* The balances in each of the major classes of fixed assets as of the end of the reporting period.
- *Depreciation expense.* The amount of depreciation charged to expense in the reporting period.
- *Depreciation methods.* A description of the methods used to depreciate assets in the major asset classifications.

For example:

> The Farm states its fixed assets at cost. For all fixed assets, the Farm calculates depreciation utilizing the straight-line method over the estimated useful lives for owned assets or, where appropriate, over the related lease terms for leasehold improvements. Useful lives range from 1 to 30 years.

> Our fixed assets include the following approximate amounts:

	December 31,	
	20X3	20X2
Buildings	$320,000	$309,000
Land	118,000	118,000
Machinery and equipment	82,000	75,000
Perennial crops	21,000	14,000
Purchased breeding livestock	24,000	20,000
Leasehold improvements	5,000	5,000
Less: Accumulated depreciation	210,000	179,000
Totals	$360,000	$362,000

> Depreciation expense was $31,000 and $29,000 in 20X3 and 20X2, respectively.

Disclosure of Deferred Income Taxes

A farm should disclose the following information in its financial statements that relates to income taxes, broken down by where the information should be disclosed.

Balance Sheet

The following information about income taxes should be disclosed within the balance sheet or the accompanying notes:

- *Carryforwards.* The amounts of all operating loss carryforwards and tax credit carryforwards, as well as their related expiration dates.
- *Deferrals.* The total of all deferred tax liabilities, the total of all deferred tax assets, and the total valuation allowance associated with the deferred tax assets. Also disclose the net change in the valuation allowance during the year.
- *Temporary differences and carryforwards.* The types of significant temporary differences and carryforwards.
- *Unrecognized tax benefits, offsetting of.* If there is an unrecognized tax benefit, present it as a reduction of any deferred tax assets for a tax credit carryforward, a net operating loss carryforward, or a similar tax loss. If there is no offset available, present the unrecognized tax benefit as a liability.

EXAMPLE

Armadillo Ranch discloses the following information about the realizability of its deferred tax assets:

> The Ranch has recorded a $50,000 deferred tax asset, which reflects the benefit to be derived from loss carryforwards. These carryforwards expire during the period 20X4 to 20X8. The realization of this tax asset is dependent upon the Ranch generating a sufficient amount of taxable income before the loss carryforwards expire. Management believes it is more likely than not that all $50,000 of the deferred tax asset will be realized.

Income Statement

The following information about income taxes should be disclosed within the income statement or the accompanying notes:

- *Comparison to statutory rate.* The nature of significant reasons why the reported income tax differs from the statutory tax rate.
- *Interest and penalties.* The amount of interest and penalties recognized in the period.
- *Tax allocations.* The income tax amount allocated to continuing operations and to other items.
- *Tax components.* The components of income taxes attributable to continuing operations, including the current tax expense, deferred tax expense, investment tax credits, government grants, benefits related to operating loss carryforwards, the tax expense resulting from the allocation of tax benefits to contributed capital, adjustments related to enacted tax laws or rates, adjustments from a change in tax status, and adjustments to the beginning valuation allowance.

EXAMPLE

Amanda Ranch discloses the following information about its income taxes in the notes accompanying its financial statements:

Current tax expense	$810
Deferred tax expense	1,240
Tax expense from continuing operations	$2,050
Tax expense at statutory rate	$2,250
Benefit of investment tax credits	-80
Benefit of operating loss carryforwards	-120
Tax expense from continuing operations	$2,050

Disclosure of Short Term Notes Payable

If a farm has a short-term debt obligation, disclose the amount of the payable, the terms of the arrangement, and the name of the lender. If a line of credit is involved, note the unused amount of the line. For example:

> The Farm has an operating line of credit with Third Agricultural Bank that is renewable on January 1 of each year. The interest rate charged is set at 1.5% above the prime rate of the bank; the rate paid by the Farm at year-end was 4.38%. The arrangement is secured by the Farm's crops. The line is capped at $260,000. A total of $162,000 and $92,000 of the line had been used as of the end of 20X3 and 20X2, respectively. This left $98,000 and $168,000 of the line unused as of the end of 20X3 and 20X2, respectively.

Disclosure of Long-Term Debt

If a farm has long-term debt obligations, disclose the amounts due in each of the next five years, as well as the aggregate amount due thereafter. Also note the terms of each debt agreement and the name of the lender. For example:

> The Farm has a 10-year borrowing arrangement with First Agricultural Bank, under which the Farm has borrowed $400,000 at a 6% interest rate, and is paying down the loan over a 10-year term. There are seven years of payments remaining on the loan. The loan is secured by the land and buildings on the farm property. That portion of the loan payable within one year is $39,000. The remaining principal payments in subsequent years are as follows:

Year ended December 31	Amount
20X4	$42,000
20X5	45,000
20X6	49,000
20X7	54,000
20X8	59,000
Thereafter	47,000
Total	$296,000

> The interest expense on the Farm's long-term debt was $29,000 and $27,000 in 20X3 and 20X2, respectively.

Disclosure of Pension Plans

If the farm has a pension plan, disclose the manner in which payments into the plan are determined, who is covered by the plan, and the amounts paid into the plan in each of the past two years. For example:

> The Farm sponsors a pension plan that covers substantially all full-time employees; this group is considered to be anyone with an average of at least 32 working hours per week. Contributions to the plan are capped at 10% of the full-year base compensation of each covered employee, with the exact amount being set by the board of directors. Contributions to the plan were $28,425 and $19,040 for the years ended December 31, 20X3 and 20X2, respectively.

These disclosures are for a defined contribution plan. The disclosures for a defined benefit plan are much more complex.

Disclosure of Investments in Cooperatives

When a farm has investments in farmers' cooperative associations, set forth in a tabular format the book value and estimated current value of these investments, including a reserve for any patronage dividends that are not expected to be collectible. For example:

Source of Patronage Dividends	Book Value	Estimated Current Value
Urban Growers Cooperative	$34,780	$21,821
Local Milk Producers	17,900	11,230
Amalgamated Livestock Cooperative	15,105	--
Total allocated patronage dividends	$67,785	$33,051
Less: Reserve for uncollectible dividends	15,105	--
Total investments in cooperatives	$52,680	$33,051

Urban Growers Cooperative and Local Milk Producers are currently operating on an eight-year revolvement of allocated patronage. To arrive at the estimated current value of these investments, the estimated current value of the investments is based on the discounted present value associated with being paid in eight years, using a 6% discount rate. Amalgamated Livestock Cooperative has not revolved patronage for the past five years and has experienced losses that have not been allocated; given the uncertainty of collection for these patronage dividends, no estimated current value can be calculated.

Disclosure of Dealings with Cooperatives

When a farm is dealing with a cooperative, the farm discloses the extent of its transactions with the cooperative if the farm is economically dependent on it for the sale of all or a significant proportion of the farm's production. For example:

> The Farm sold 82% and 79% of its production to the Producers Crop Marketing Association during the years ended December 31, 20X3 and 20X2, respectively.

Summary

The disclosures attached to the financial statements can provide readers with at least as much information as the numerical content in the basic financial statements. Consequently, the farm accountant should spend a significant amount of time to ensure that each topic has been thoroughly and accurately disclosed.

Despite the number of disclosures noted in this chapter, the material presented is actually an abbreviated version of the full detail that may be required, depending on the circumstances. For a comprehensive discussion of disclosures, see the author's *GAAP Guidebook*.

Chapter 18
Farm Financial Analysis

Introduction

The bulk of this book covers the *accounting* for farms. Once the accounting information has been assembled into financial statements, it can be reviewed to see how well a farm is performing. This can be accomplished with horizontal analysis and a number of ratios and other measurements, which are discussed in the following sections.

Horizontal Analysis

One of the essential tools for reviewing the performance of a farm is horizontal analysis. This is the comparison of historical financial information over a series of reporting periods, or of the ratios derived from this information. The analysis is most commonly a simple grouping of information that is sorted by period, but the numbers in each succeeding period can also be expressed as a percentage of the amount in the baseline year, with the baseline amount being listed as 100%.

When conducting a horizontal analysis, it is useful to do so for all of the financial statements at the same time, in order to see the complete impact of operational results on the farm's financial condition over the review period. For example, as noted in the next two illustrations, the income statement analysis shows a farm having an excellent second year, but the related balance sheet analysis shows that it is having trouble funding growth, given the decline in cash, increase in accounts payable, and increase in debt.

Horizontal analysis of the income statement is usually in a two-year format such as the one shown next, with a variance also reported that states the difference between the two years for each line item. An alternative format is to simply add as many years as will fit on the page, without showing a variance, in order to see general changes by account over multiple years.

Income Statement Horizontal Analysis

	20X1	20X2	Variance
Sales	$1,000,000	$1,500,000	$500,000
Feeder livestock	600,000	900,000	-300,000
Gross margin	400,000	600,000	200,000
Wage expense	250,000	375,000	-125,000
Interest expense	50,000	80,000	-30,000
Supplies expense	10,000	20,000	-10,000
Utilities expense	20,000	30,000	-10,000
Other expenses	30,000	50,000	-20,000
Total expenses	360,000	555,000	-195,000
Net profit	$40,000	$45,000	$5,000

Horizontal analysis of the balance sheet is also usually in a two-year format, such as the one shown next, with a variance stating the difference between the two years for each line item. An alternative format is to add as many years as will fit on the page, without showing a variance, in order to see general changes by line item over multiple years.

Balance Sheet Horizontal Analysis

	20X1	20X2	Variance
Cash	$100,000	$80,000	-$20,000
Accounts receivable	350,000	525,000	175,000
Inventory - livestock	150,000	275,000	125,000
Total current assets	600,000	880,000	280,000
Fixed assets	400,000	800,000	400,000
Total assets	$1,000,000	$1,680,000	$680,000
Accounts payable	$180,000	$300,000	$120,000
Accrued liabilities	70,000	120,000	50,000
Total current liabilities	250,000	420,000	170,000
Notes payable	300,000	525,000	225,000
Total liabilities	550,000	945,000	395,000
Retained capital	450,000	735,000	285,000
Total liabilities and equity	$1,000,000	$1,680,000	$680,000

188

The easiest way to use horizontal analysis is to scan across each line, looking for unusual spikes or dips in the numbers. Only investigate material changes, which will probably only comprise a small proportion of the total amount of presented numbers. By taking this approach, the farm manager can pursue those issues that are worthy of his time and avoid becoming bogged down in the investigation of minor items in the financial statements.

If the information in a horizontal analysis is converted into percentage changes from the base year, it is easy to be misled by a large percentage that is related to a relatively minor item. For example, if the tools expense was $6,000 in the base year and then increased by 20%, the size of this increase might cause the farm manager to spend an inordinate amount of time tracking down the reason for the change – even though the total amount of the change was only $1,200. Thus, be aware of the underlying dollar value of a percentage change before conducting a detailed investigation.

Financial Ratio Analysis

A financial ratio is a comparison of two or more values taken from a farm's financial statements. These ratios can be used to compare the condition of a farm from one year to the next, or to compare it to the condition of other farms in the area. When tracked on a trend line, these ratios can be quite effective in determining patterns in the financial condition of a business.

There are several hundred ratios that could be used to evaluate a farm. A small proportion of these ratios are sufficient for ascertaining most of the issues that a farm may have. Those ratios can be clustered into a few groups, each of which provides different types of financial information. The main clusters are performance ratios, efficiency ratios, liquidity ratios, and return on investment ratios. They are described in the following sections.

Performance Ratios

Performance ratios are used to evaluate the information on a farm's income statement. They quantify the proportions of income being generated by different aspects of a farm. These measures can also be used to evaluate the quality of earnings and how closely a farm is operating to its breakeven level.

Net Profit Ratio

The net profit ratio is a comparison of after-tax profits to sales. It reveals the remaining profits after *all* costs have been deducted from sales and income taxes recognized. As such, it is one of the best measures of the overall results of a farm. The measure is commonly reported on a trend line, to judge performance over time. It is also used to compare the results of a farm to those of its competitors.

The net profit ratio is really a short-term measurement, because a farm manager may delay a variety of discretionary expenses, such as maintenance, to make the net profit ratio look better than it normally is. Consequently, evaluate this ratio alongside an array of other metrics to gain a full picture of a farm's ability to continue as a going concern.

Another issue with the net profit ratio is that a farm manager may intentionally keep it low through a variety of expense recognition strategies in order to avoid paying taxes. If so, review the statement of cash flows to determine the real cash-generating ability of the business.

To calculate the net profit ratio, divide net profits by net sales and then multiply by 100. The formula is:

$$(\text{Net profit} \div \text{Net sales}) \times 100$$

EXAMPLE

Keeper Farm has $100,000 of sales in its most recent month, and production and other operating costs of $96,000. The income tax rate is 35%. The calculation of its net profit percentage is:

$$\$100,000 \text{ Sales} - \$96,000 \text{ Expenses}$$

$$= \$4,000 \text{ Income before tax}$$

$$\$4,000 \text{ Income before tax} \times (1 - 0.35) = \$2,600 \text{ Profit after tax}$$

$$(\$2,600 \text{ Profit after tax} \div \$100,000 \text{ Net Sales}) \times 100$$

$$= 2.6\% \text{ Net profit ratio}$$

Operating Income Ratio

The standard performance measurement for any business is the net profit ratio, but that ratio suffers from the inclusion of one-time and non-operating gains and losses. For example, there may be an insurance loss and investment income – neither of which reveals the true state of the underlying farm operations. A way to discern the underlying level of profitability is to use the operating income ratio, which compares operating income to only those sales related to operations. To calculate the operating income ratio, follow these steps:

1. Clean up the sales figure by eliminating any "sales" transactions that are really interest income or one-time gains.
2. Clean up the net profit ratio by eliminating all financing-related interest and income, as well as gains and losses on one-time transactions. The result is operating income.
3. Divide the operating income figure by the adjusted sales figure.

The formulation of the operating income ratio is:

$$\frac{\text{Net profit} - \text{Non-operating gain and loss transactions}}{\text{Sales} - \text{Non-operating transactions recorded as sales}}$$

EXAMPLE

Amalgamated Farms raised $100 million in a private stock placement two years ago, with the intent of using the money to buy up a large amount of ranch land. Amalgamated has reported net profits of $4,500,000 and $5,200,000 in the following two years, but this may be masking losses that are being netted against interest income on the $100 million of cash. An investor quizzes the controller about this issue, and learns that $4,200,000 and $3,100,000 of interest income have been recorded as revenue in the past two years. Total revenues reported were $62,000,000 and $67,000,000, respectively, in years 1 and 2. The following table eliminates the interest income to arrive at the company's operating income ratio:

	Year 1	Year 2
Reported revenue	$62,000,000	$67,000,000
Less: Interest income	-4,200,000	-3,900,000
Adjusted revenue	$57,800,000	$63,100,000
Reported net profits	$4,500,000	$5,200,000
Less: Interest income	-4,200,000	-3,900,000
Operating income	$300,000	$1,300,000
Operating income ratio	0.5%	2.1%

The ratio reveals that most of the income reported by Amalgamated has really been derived from its investment of the $100 million of cash, rather than from operations. However, the situation appears to be improving, since the operating profit quadrupled in Year 2.

Quality of Earnings Ratio

The "real" performance of a farm equates to the cash flows that it generates, irrespective of the results that appear in its income statement. Any number of accruals and aggressive or conservative interpretations of the accounting standards can lead to a wide divergence between the reported amounts of cash flows and net income. The greater the divergence, the more an observer must wonder about the reliability of the information being presented. This issue is addressed by the quality of earnings ratio, which compares the reported level of earnings to reported cash flows. Earnings are considered to be of high quality if the two figures are relatively close to each other.

To calculate the quality of earnings, follow these steps:

1. Obtain the "Cash from operations" line item in the statement of cash flows.
2. Subtract the cash from operations figure from the net profit figure in the income statement.
3. Divide the result by the average asset figure for the business during the measurement period.

The formula is:

$$\frac{\text{Net profits} - \text{Cash from operations}}{\text{Average assets}}$$

An occasional spike in this ratio can be explained by a farm accountant's compliance with the accounting standards in regard to a specific issue, and can be entirely legitimate. However, if the amount of net profits is persistently higher than cash from operations for a number of reporting periods, it is likely that management is actively engaged in the inflation of the net profits figure.

EXAMPLE

The Red Herring Ranch has been having difficulty meeting its loan covenants over the past few months, and the bank's loan officer is beginning to suspect that something fishy is going on. She reviews the ranch's latest set of financial statements and extracts the following information:

Cash from operations	$2,300,000
Net profits	4,700,000
Beginning assets	11,000,000
Ending assets	11,400,000

Based on this information, she compiles the following quality of earnings ratio:

$$\frac{\$4,700,000 \text{ Net profits} - \$2,300,000 \text{ Cash from operations}}{(\$11,000,000 \text{ Beginning assets} - \$11,400,000 \text{ Ending assets}) \div 2}$$

$$= 21\%$$

The ratio reveals quite a substantial difference between the cash flows and reported (and possibly inflated) earnings of Red Herring. The loan officer decides that it is time to send in an audit team to review the ranch's books.

Breakeven Point

The breakeven point is the sales volume at which a farm earns exactly no money. It is useful for deciding how close to the edge of failure a farm is operating, based on its current sales level.

To calculate the breakeven point, divide total fixed expenses by the contribution margin of the farm. Contribution margin is sales minus all variable expenses, divided by sales. The formula is:

$$\frac{\text{Total fixed expenses}}{\text{Contribution margin percentage}}$$

A more refined approach is to eliminate all non-cash expenses (such as depreciation) from the numerator, so that the calculation focuses on the breakeven cash flow level.

EXAMPLE

A credit analyst is reviewing the financial statements of a farm that has a large amount of fixed costs. The industry is highly cyclical, so the analyst wants to know what a large downturn in sales will do to the farm. The farm has total fixed expenses of $300,000, sales of $800,000, and variable expenses of $400,000. Based on this information, the farm's contribution margin is 50%. The breakeven calculation is:

$$\frac{\$300,000 \text{ Total fixed costs}}{50\% \text{ Contribution margin}}$$

$$= \$600,000 \text{ Breakeven sales level}$$

Thus, the farm's sales can decline by $200,000 from their current level before it will begin to lose money.

Efficiency Ratios

Efficiency ratios are derived from the balance sheet, and are targeted at the amount of assets that a farm is using in order to generate a certain amount of sales. In the following sub-sections, we describe efficiency ratios for assets in general and for working capital in particular.

Asset Turnover Ratio

The asset turnover ratio compares the revenues of a farm to its average assets. The measure is used to estimate the efficiency with which the farm manager uses assets to produce sales. A high turnover level indicates that a farm uses a minimal amount of working capital and fixed assets in its daily operations. To calculate the ratio, divide sales by total average assets.

The average assets figure is derived by adding together the beginning and ending asset totals for the measurement period and dividing by two. The formula is:

$$\frac{\text{Revenue}}{(\text{Beginning assets} + \text{Ending assets}) \div 2}$$

EXAMPLE

Sunrise Farm has sales of $1,000,000, beginning total assets of $200,000 and ending total assets of $300,000. Its asset turnover ratio is:

$$\frac{\$1,000,000 \text{ Revenue}}{(\$200,000 \text{ Beginning assets} + \$300,000 \text{ Ending assets}) \div 2}$$

$$= 4:1 \text{ Asset turnover ratio}$$

In short, the farm is generating $4 of sales for every $1 of assets.

This ratio can be useful for comparing the results of different farms, especially to see if any farms are operating outside of the median turnover level for the group.

Working Capital Turnover

The working capital turnover ratio measures how well a farm is utilizing its working capital to support a given level of sales. Working capital is current assets minus current liabilities. A high turnover ratio indicates that the farm manager is being extremely efficient in using short-term assets and liabilities to support sales. Conversely, a low ratio indicates that a farm is investing in too many accounts receivable and inventory assets to support its sales.

To calculate the ratio, divide sales by working capital (which is current assets minus current liabilities). The calculation is usually made on an annual or trailing 12-month basis, and uses the average working capital during that period. The calculation is:

$$\frac{\text{Sales}}{(\text{Beginning working capital} + \text{Ending working capital}) \div 2}$$

EXAMPLE

Woodbine Farm had $1,200,000 of sales over the past twelve months, and average working capital during that period of $200,000. The calculation of its working capital turnover ratio is:

$$\frac{\$1,200,000 \text{ Sales}}{\$200,000 \text{ Average working capital}}$$

$$= 6.0 \text{ Working capital turnover ratio}$$

An extremely high working capital turnover ratio can indicate that a farm does not have enough capital to support it sales; collapse of the farm may be imminent. This is a particularly strong indicator when the accounts payable component of working capital is very high, since it indicates that the farm cannot pay its bills as they come due for payment.

An excessively high turnover ratio can be spotted by comparing the ratio for a particular farm to those reported for a group of similar farms, to see if the business is reporting outlier results.

Liquidity Ratios

These ratios are used to discern whether a farm can meet its payable and debt obligations as they become due for payment. These ratios are particularly important for a farm, which may be operating under a substantial debt load. We present five liquidity ratios in this section.

Current Ratio

One of the first ratios that a lender or supplier reviews when examining a farm is its current ratio. The current ratio measures the short-term liquidity of a business; that is, it gives an indication of the ability of a farm to pay its bills. A ratio of 2:1 is preferred, with a lower proportion indicating a reduced ability to pay in a timely manner. Since the ratio is current assets divided by current liabilities, the ratio essentially implies that current assets can be liquidated to pay for current liabilities.

To calculate the current ratio, divide the total of all current assets by the total of all current liabilities. The formula is:

$$\frac{\text{Current assets}}{\text{Current liabilities}}$$

The current ratio can yield misleading results under the following circumstances:

- *Inventory component.* When the current assets figure includes a large proportion of inventory assets, since these assets can be difficult to liquidate, especially if the farm manager is holding them to see if prices will escalate in the future.
- *Paying from debt.* When a farm is drawing upon its line of credit to pay bills as they come due, which means that the cash balance is near zero. In this case, the current ratio could be fairly low, and yet the presence of a line of credit still allows a farm to pay its suppliers in a timely manner.

EXAMPLE

A supplier wants to learn about the financial condition of Willow Farms. The supplier calculates the current ratio of Willow for the past three years:

	Year 1	Year 2	Year 3
Current assets	$800,000	$1,640,000	$2,340,000
Current liabilities	$400,000	$965,000	$1,800,000
Current ratio	2:1	1.7:1	1.3:1

The sudden rise in current assets over the past two years indicates that Willow has undergone a rapid expansion of its operations. Of particular concern is the increase in accounts payable in Year 3, which indicates a rapidly deteriorating ability to pay suppliers. Based on this information, the supplier elects to restrict the extension of credit to Willow.

Cash Ratio

The cash ratio compares the most liquid assets to current liabilities, to determine if a farm can meet its short-term obligations. It is the most conservative of all the liquidity measurements, since it excludes inventory and accounts receivable.

To calculate the cash ratio, add together cash and cash equivalents (highly liquid investments maturing in less than three months), and divide by current liabilities. A variation that may be slightly more accurate is to exclude accrued expenses from the current liabilities in the denominator, since it may not be necessary to pay for these items in the near term. The calculation is:

$$\frac{\text{Cash} + \text{Cash equivalents}}{\text{Current liabilities}}$$

If a farm wants to show a high cash ratio to the outside world, it must keep a large amount of cash on hand as of the measurement date, probably more than is prudent. Another issue is that the ratio only measures cash balances as of a specific point in time, which may vary considerably on a daily basis as receivables are collected and suppliers are paid. Further, the ratio essentially assumes that the cash on hand now will be used to pay for all accounts payable, when in reality the cash from an ongoing series of receivable payments will also be used.

EXAMPLE

Missionary Ridge Ranch has $10,000 of cash and $40,000 of cash equivalents on its balance sheet at the end of May. On that date, its current liabilities are $100,000. Its cash ratio is:

$$\frac{\$10,000 \text{ Cash} + \$40,000 \text{ Cash equivalents}}{\$100,000 \text{ Current liabilities}}$$

$$= 0.5{:}1 \text{ Cash ratio}$$

Debt to Equity Ratio

The debt to equity ratio of a farm is closely monitored by its lenders and creditors, since the ratio can provide early warning that an organization is so overwhelmed by debt that it is unable to meet its payment obligations. This may also be triggered by a funding issue. For example, the owners of a farm may not want to contribute any more cash to the business, so they acquire more debt to address a cash shortfall.

Whatever the reason for debt usage, the outcome can be catastrophic if cash flows are not sufficient to make ongoing debt payments. This is a concern to lenders, whose loans may not be paid back. Suppliers are also concerned about the ratio for the same reason. A lender can protect its interests by imposing collateral requirements or restrictive covenants; suppliers usually offer credit with less restrictive terms, and so can suffer more if a farm is unable to meet its payment obligations to them.

To calculate the debt to equity ratio, simply divide total debt by total equity. In this calculation, the debt figure should also include all lease obligations. The formula is:

$$\frac{\text{Long-term debt} + \text{Short-term debt} + \text{Leases}}{\text{Equity}}$$

EXAMPLE

An analyst is reviewing the credit application of New Century Farm. The farm reports a $500,000 line of credit, $1,700,000 in long-term debt, and a $200,000 lease. The farm has $800,000 of equity. Based on this information, New Century's debt to equity ratio is:

$$\frac{\$500,000 \text{ Line of credit} + \$1,700,000 \text{ Debt} + \$200,000 \text{ Lease}}{\$800,000 \text{ Equity}}$$

$$= 3{:}1 \text{ Debt to equity ratio}$$

The debt to equity ratio exceeds the 2:1 ratio threshold above which the analyst is not allowed to grant credit. Consequently, New Century is kept on cash-in-advance payment terms.

Debt Service Coverage Ratio

The debt service coverage ratio measures the ability of a revenue-producing property to generate sufficient cash to pay for the cost of all related mortgage payments. A positive debt service ratio indicates that a property's cash outflows can cover all off-setting loan payments, whereas a negative ratio indicates that the owner must contribute additional funds to pay for the annual loan payments. A very high debt service coverage ratio gives the property owner a substantial cushion to pay for unexpected or unplanned expenditures related to the property, or if market conditions result in a significant decline in future cash flows.

To calculate the ratio, divide the net annual operating income of the property by all annual loan payments for the same property, net of any tax savings generated by the interest expense. The formula is:

$$\frac{\text{Net annual operating income}}{\text{Total of annual loan payments net of tax effect}}$$

There may be no tax effect associated with debt, if a farm has no taxable income. Otherwise, the tax effect is based on the income tax rate expected for the year.

EXAMPLE

A farm property generates $400,000 of cash flow per year, and the total annual loan payments of the property are $360,000. This yields a debt service ratio of 1.11, meaning that the property generates 11% more cash than the owner needs to pay for the annual loan payments.

Capital Debt Repayment Capacity

The owners of a farm may have taken on a substantial amount of debt in order to finance farm operations. If so, the lender will likely want to calculate the capital debt repayment capacity of the farm, to see if it can throw off enough cash to pay off its debt. The calculation needed to arrive at the debt repayment capacity is as follows:

+	Net farm income from operations
+/-	Total miscellaneous revenues/expenses
+	Total non-farm income
+	Depreciation expense
-	Income tax expense
-	Owner withdrawals
+	Interest expense on term debt
=	Capital debt repayment capacity

EXAMPLE

Sunset Farms has reported $25,000 of net farm income from operations. A review of its combined year-end financial statements reveals the following additional information:

- $12,000 of non-farm income
- $4,000 of depreciation expense
- $6,000 of income tax expense
- $18,000 of interest expense
- $7,000 of owner withdrawals

The resulting capital debt repayment capacity of the farm is:

+	$25,000 Net farm income from operations
+	$12,000 Non-farm income
+	$4,000 Depreciation expense
-	$6,000 Income tax expense
-	$7,000 Owner withdrawals
+	$18,000 Interest expense on term debt
=	$46,000 Capital debt repayment capacity

Return on Investment Ratios

Over the long term, the owners of a farm should have a keen interest in the return being generated from the property. If the return is not adequate, they may want to find an alternative use for their invested funds. In this section, we cover the two most common measures of the return on investment, which are the return on equity and the return on assets.

Return on Equity

The return on equity (ROE) ratio reveals the amount of return earned by investors on their investments in a farm. It is one of the metrics most closely watched by investors. ROE is essentially net income divided by shareholders' equity. ROE performance can be enhanced by focusing on improvements to three underlying measurements, all of which roll up into ROE. These sub-level measurements are:

- *Profit margin.* Calculated as net income divided by sales. Can be improved by trimming expenses, increasing prices, or altering the mix of products sold.
- *Asset turnover.* Calculated as sales divided by assets. Can be improved by reducing receivable balances, inventory levels, and/or the investment in fixed assets, as well as by lengthening payables payment terms.
- *Financial leverage.* Calculated as assets divided by shareholders' equity. Can be improved by buying back shares (if the farm is structured as a corporation), paying dividends, or using more debt to fund operations.

Or, stated as a formula, the return on equity is as follows:

Return on Equity	=	$\dfrac{\text{Net income}}{\text{Sales}}$	×	$\dfrac{\text{Sales}}{\text{Assets}}$	×	$\dfrac{\text{Assets}}{\text{Shareholders' equity}}$

EXAMPLE

Colton Creek Farms' return on equity has declined from a high of 25% five years ago to a current level of 10%. The farm manager wants to know what is causing the problem, and assigns the task to Wendy, the farm accountant. She reviews the components of ROE for both periods, and derives the following information:

	ROE		Profit Margin		Asset Turnover		Financial Leverage
Five Years Ago	25%	=	12%	×	1.2x	×	1.75x
Today	10%	=	10%	×	0.6x	×	1.70x

The information in the table reveals that the primary culprit causing the decline is a sharp reduction in the farm's asset turnover. This has been caused by a large buildup in the farm's inventory levels, which have been caused by the farm manager's persistent belief that corn stocks should be held for long periods of time to see if the price will increase based on forthcoming government trade deals with other countries that will increase demand.

The multiple components of the ROE calculation present an opportunity for a farm to generate a high ROE in several ways. For example, if a farm has low profits on a per-unit basis, but grows several crops per year, it can earn a profit on many sale transactions over the course of a year. Conversely, a farm may earn large profits on each per-unit sale but can grow only one or two crops per year. The following illustration shows how both entities can earn an identical ROE, despite having such a different emphasis on profits and asset turnover. In the illustration, we ignore the effects of financial leverage.

Comparison of Returns on Equity

	ROE		Profit Margin		Asset Turnover
Low margin, many crops	20%	=	2%	×	10x
High margin, few crops	20%	=	40%	×	0.5x

A high level of financial leverage can increase the return on equity, because it means a farm is using the minimum possible amount of equity, instead relying on debt to fund its operations. By doing so, the amount of equity in the denominator of the return on equity equation is minimized. If any profits are generated by funding activities with debt, these changes are added to the numerator in the equation, thereby increasing the return on equity.

The trouble with employing financial leverage is that it imposes a new fixed expense in the form of interest payments. If sales decline, this added cost of debt could trigger a steep decline in profits that could end in bankruptcy. Thus, a farm that relies too much on debt to enhance its owner returns may find itself in significant financial trouble. A more prudent path is to employ a modest amount of additional debt that a farm can comfortably handle even through a business downturn.

A case can be made that ROE should be ignored, since an excessive focus on it may drive the farm manager to pare back on a number of discretionary expenses that are needed to build the long-term value of a farm. For example, he could cut back on essential maintenance or equipment upgrades, as well as experimentation in the use of new crops, in order to boost profits in the short term and elevate ROE. However, doing so impairs the ability of the farm to maintain or increase its profits over the long term.

Return on Assets

The return on assets measurement focuses on the amount and usage level of the assets employed by a farm. To increase the return on assets, there is a built-in incentive to either eliminate nonproductive assets or increase asset usage. The formula is:

$$\frac{\text{Net income}}{\text{Total assets}}$$

The measurement is certainly a simple one, but its all-encompassing nature also means that the result may not yield the type of information needed. Consider the following issues:

- *Non-operating income*. The numerator of the ratio is net income, which includes income from all sources, some of which may not be even remotely related to the assets of the business. For example, net income may include one-time gains or losses from hedging activities, as well as interest income or expense. This issue can be avoided by only using operating income in the numerator.
- *Tax rate*. The net income figure is net of the farm's income tax liability. This liability is a result of the farm accountant's tax strategy, which may yield an inordinately low (or high) tax rate. Also, depending on the tax strategy, the tax rate could change markedly from year to year. Because of the effect of tax planning, a non-operational technical issue could have a major impact on the calculated amount of return on assets. This concern can be sidestepped by only using before-tax information in the measurement.
- *Cash basis*. The net income figure can be significantly skewed if a farm operates on the cash basis of accounting, where transactions are recorded when cash is received or paid out. This issue can be avoided by only using the measurement on a farm that employs the accrual basis of accounting.
- *Cash holdings*. The total assets figure in the denominator includes *all* assets; this means that a farm with a significant amount of undistributed cash reserves

will reveal a lower return on assets, simply because it has not chosen to employ the cash. This issue can be avoided by subtracting cash from the total assets figure in the measurement, or by using a cash amount considered sufficient to support the ongoing operations of the farm.

Given these problems, we suggest an alternative measurement, which uses operating income in the numerator and subtracts all cash from the denominator. The formula is:

$$\frac{\text{Operating income}}{\text{Total assets - Cash}}$$

EXAMPLE

Barker Ridge Farms has net income of $200,000, which includes a one-time hedging loss of $30,000. The farm has assets of $1,100,000, of which $150,000 is excess cash that the owning family intends to extract in the form of an owner withdrawal. For the purposes of calculating Barker's return on assets, the hedging loss is added back to the net income figure, while the $150,000 of excess cash is subtracted from its total assets figure. The resulting calculation is:

$$\frac{\$230,000 \text{ Adjusted income}}{\$950,000 \text{ Assets net of excess cash}}$$

$$= 24.2\% \text{ Return on assets}$$

A further issue with the return on assets is that net farm income (as explained in the next section) does not include the wage cost of the family owning a farm. To get a better idea of the return on assets, consider adding back to income the amount of owner withdrawals for unpaid labor and management time. This figure may be only an approximation of wage costs, but is better than not including the family's wage costs in the calculation at all.

Net Farm Income

A special item for consideration is net farm income, which is the revenue of a farm minus all production costs and any gains and losses from the disposal of fixed assets. It is frequently used to evaluate the profitability of a farm. The problem is that the family owning a farm does not record the cost of its wages in the financial statements of the farm; this expense is not recognized when the farm is operated as a sole proprietorship. Consequently, net farm income needs to be quite high in order to cover this significant additional expense (that is, provide an adequate living for the farm family). Further, net farm income should represent a reasonable return to the farm family on the funds it has invested in the business.

A further problem with the non-inclusion of farm family wages in net farm income is that the resulting profit figure cannot be compared with the reported profit levels in other industries, since most other industries *do* include this compensation, and therefore have lower reported profit levels.

The Farm Financial Standards Council does not recommend that a farm family charge its own wages through the farm income statement, since there is no guarantee that the amounts charged actually reflect the local wage rates.

If the farm manager wants to include family wages in a separate version of the income statement, we suggest that this be done, but only to evaluate whether the farm is generating a sufficient return. This version should not be used for external reporting, such as to a creditor or lender.

EBITDA

A good way to arrive at an approximation of the operational cash flows of a farm is to calculate its earnings before interest, taxes, depreciation, and amortization (EBITDA). This measurement removes financial considerations (interest expense), income taxes, and non-cash items (depreciation and amortization) from farm earnings. What remains may come close to matching the actual cash flows of the business. However, EBITDA and actual cash flows will not exactly match, since cash flows are not influenced by accrual-basis accounting entries, and because EBITDA does not include the cash flows associated with the purchase or sale of fixed assets.

Despite these issues, if a farm has not issued a statement of cash flows, a quick EBITDA calculation can be used to arrive at something relatively close to a cash flow number. Also, the EBITDA figure provides an estimate of the amount of funds available to pay for a farm's debt.

EXAMPLE

Emerson Farms reports net profit of $82,000 for the past year. The farm's income statement includes the following information:

- Interest expense was $11,000
- Income tax expense was $27,000
- Depreciation expense was $14,000

Based on this information, Emerson's EBITDA was $134,000, which is calculated as follows:

+	$82,000 Net profit
+	11,000 Interest expense
+	27,000 Income tax expense
+	14,000 Depreciation expense
=	$134,000 EBITDA

Livestock Analysis Formulas

The focus of this chapter has been on financial analysis, which means examining the financial statements of a farm. In addition, we include in the following table several formulas that may be of use to those people managing livestock.

Livestock Analysis Formulas

Formula Name	Formula Calculation
Average daily gain	(Ending weight – starting weight) ÷ number of days of growth
Feed cost per animal	Pounds of feed fed per animal ÷ price of feed per pound
Feed cost per pound of gain	Feed cost per animal ÷ total weight gain
Feed per pound of gain	Total pounds of feed consumed per animal ÷ total weight gain
Total weight gain	Ending weight – starting weight

Summary

A simple perusal of a farm's financial statements may not result in a person learning much, for the presented information is highly aggregated and is spread across multiple reports. The financial analysis tools presented in this chapter can assist in deriving a better understanding of a farm's financial situation. Horizontal analysis is highly recommended for spotting anomalies in the most recent financial statements, while the various ratios are designed to present comparisons between some of the more significant line items in the financial statements. The ratios noted in this chapter are only some of the possibilities available; the farm manager should certainly consider adding other measurements that are more specific to his operations.

Chapter 19
The Farmer's Tax Guide

Introduction

The federal government has given significant tax breaks to the agricultural sector, which are spread across a broad range of tax areas. All tax areas applicable to agriculture are summarized in Publication 225, *Farmer's Tax Guide*, which is regularly updated by the Internal Revenue Service. In this chapter, we summarize the major areas of the *Guide*, but do not offer specific tax advice. Instead, you should consult the most recent release of the *Guide* and also confer with your tax accountant.

Major Sections of the Farmer's Tax Guide

In this section, we cover the contents of the major sections of the *Farmer's Tax Guide*. This summarization can be useful in drilling down through the actual *Guide* (which is readily available on the Internet as a PDF download – just do a Google search on "Farmer's Tax Guide." The main topics are as follows:

- *What's New*. Always check this section, which is located near the front of the *Guide*. It enumerates any changes to farm-related taxes during the past year.
- *Importance of Records*. This is a boilerplate section that emphasizes the need to maintain proper accounting records. There is an emphasis on recordkeeping for a variety of expenses, employment taxes, excise taxes, and assets.
- *Accounting Methods*. This section describes the cash and accrual methods of accounting, and notes the methods available for calculating the value of farm inventory.
- *Farm Income*. This section describes the different types of farm income, including sales caused by weather-related conditions, rent received, agricultural program payments, income from cooperatives, and the cancellation of debt. The coverage in this section is extensive.
- *Farm Business Expenses*. This section describes a variety of expenses that can be deducted, including repairs and maintenance, breeding fees, fertilizer and lime, insurance, and depreciation. This section is worth a close read.
- *Soil and Water Conservation Expenses*. This section covers the deductions that are available for soil or water conservation, the prevention of erosion to land used in farming, or the recovery of endangered species.
- *Basis of Assets*. This section covers the farmer's basis of assets, which is the amount invested in property for tax purposes. It is used to calculate the gain or loss on the sale, exchange, or other disposition of property.

- *Depreciation, Depletion, and Amortization*. This section describes the different types of depreciation, depletion, and amortization that are available for tax deductions, as well as Section 179 property deductions.
- *Gains and Losses*. This section describes the situations in which a taxable gain or loss must be reported, and how to calculate it.
- *Dispositions of Property Used in Farming*. This section describes the tax treatment of farming property that has been disposed of, as well as the need for depreciation recapture for this property.
- *Installment Sales*. This section describes the tax impact of installment sales, where you receive at least one payment after the tax year of a sale. It is used for the reporting of gains on these types of sales.
- *Casualties, Thefts, and Condemnations*. This catchall section covers the tax impact of a variety of loss situations. Pay particular attention to the discussion of disaster area losses.
- *Self-Employment Tax*. This section covers who needs to pay self-employment tax, and how to calculate it.
- *Employment Taxes*. This section describes the types of employment taxes and who is covered by them.
- *Fuel Excise Tax Credits and Refunds*. This section describes the fuels used in farming, and how to claim a credit or refund for any expenditures related to them.
- *Estimated Tax*. This section covers the payment of estimated taxes, which are required for any income that is not subject to withholding.

Of the preceding sections, the ones containing information most useful to the bulk of a farmer's tax return will be the farm income and farm business expenses sections, though many of the other sections may contain nuggets that can potentially reduce one's tax burden.

Summary

The tax rules laid out in the *Guide* can seem overwhelming, especially for people with minimal tax experience. Many state Cooperative Extension Services conduct farm tax workshops in conjunction with the IRS. Contact your county or regional extension office for more information. Another source of information is the Rural Tax Education website, located at www.ruraltax.org.

Glossary

A

Accelerated depreciation. The depreciation of fixed assets at a very fast rate early in their useful lives.

Account. A record in an accounting system.

Accounting. The systematic recordation of the transactions of a business.

Accounting equation. The concept that assets in the balance sheet should equal liabilities plus equity.

Accrual. A journal entry that is used to recognize revenues and expenses that have been earned or consumed, respectively, but for which the related source documents have not yet been received or generated.

Accrual basis accounting. A method of recording accounting transactions for revenue when earned and expenses when incurred.

Accrued expenses. An expense that has been incurred, but for which there is not yet any expenditure documentation.

Accumulated depreciation. The to-date amount of depreciation charged against an asset.

Adjusting entry. A journal entry that is used at the end of an accounting period to adjust the balance in a general ledger account.

Advances. Amounts paid to patrons prior to final settlement.

Agricultural cooperative. Any association in which farmers act together to process, prepare for market, and market their products. The organization does less than half of its business with nonmembers.

Agricultural producer. A farmer or rancher. Examples of their activities are breeding and feeding livestock, as well as raising crops.

Amortization. The write-off of an intangible asset over its expected period of use.

Amortization schedule. A table that states the periodic payments to be made as part of a loan agreement, including the interest and principal components of each payment.

Annuals. Field and row crops that have a growing cycle of not more than one year.

Assigned amounts. The amounts used to record the products that patrons have delivered to a marketing cooperative that is operating on a pooling basis. This also refers to the patron liability if the amounts to be paid are calculated when the pool is closed. The pricing for these assigned amounts may be based on the prices currently being paid by other buyers, or by the board of directors of the cooperative.

Available-for-sale security. A security that is not classified as a trading security or a held-to-maturity security.

B

Bad debt. An invoice for which payment is not expected.

Balance sheet. A financial statement that presents information about an entity's assets, liabilities, and shareholders' equity.

Bank balance. The cash balance in an account, as reported by the bank.

Bank reconciliation. A document that shows the differences between a farm's cash records and those of its bank.

Bargaining cooperative. A cooperative that negotiates with processors on behalf of its members.

Base value method. A method for assigning costs to livestock that is derived from a cost acquired from a reputable source.

Book value. The original cost of an asset, minus any accumulated depreciation and impairment charges.

Breeding herd. Both mature and immature animals that are maintained for their progeny.

C

Capitalization limit. The amount paid for an asset, above which it is recorded as a fixed asset.

Carryback. The application of a tax loss to a prior period.

Carryforward. The application of a tax loss to a future period.

Cash basis accounting. A method of recording accounting transactions for revenue when cash is received and expenses when cash is paid.

Chart of accounts. A list of all accounts used by an entity.

Commercial production. The initial point at which production from a grove, orchard, or vineyard begins to make operations economically feasible, based on expected price points.

Comprehensive income. The change in equity of a business during a period, not including investments by or distributions to owners.

Contra account. An account that offsets the balance in another account with which it is paired.

Contribution. Revenue minus all variable expenses.

Creditor. A business that allows a customer to pay bills on a later date, without paying interest.

Crop development costs. Those costs incurred until the time when crops are produced in commercial quantities. These costs include the costs of land preparation, plants, planting, fertilization, grafting, pruning, equipment use, and irrigation.

Crops. Berries, fibers, fruits, grains, nuts, and vegetables grown by an agricultural producer.

Current asset. An asset that is cash, or which will be converted into cash within one year.

Current liability. A liability that will be settled within one year.

D

Debt security. A debt instrument that can be bought and sold.

Deferred tax expense. The net change in the deferred tax liabilities and tax assets of a business during a period of time.

Defined benefit plan. An employee benefit plan in which the payments from the plan to beneficiaries are fixed.

Defined contribution plan. An employee benefit plan in which the payments into the plan are fixed.

Depreciation. The systematic reduction in the recorded cost of a fixed asset.

Derivative financial instrument. A financial contract whose value depends on the price of an underlying asset or benchmark.

Direct write-off method. The practice of charging an unpaid invoice to expense only when it is apparent that payment will not be received.

Double-entry accounting. A method of recording transactions that requires the recordation of at least one debit and credit for each transaction.

E

Equity. The net amount of funds invested in a business by its owners, plus any retained earnings.

Equity security. An ownership position in another business.

Exempt cooperative. A cooperative that can declare a tax deduction for a limited amount paid as dividends on capital stock and distributions to patrons of income derived from business with the U.S. government and non-patronage income.

Expense. The reduction in value of an asset as it is used to create revenue.

F

Fair value hedge. A hedge of the exposure to changes in the fair value of an asset or liability that is attributable to a specific risk.

Feeder livestock. Cattle, lambs, or pigs being fattened in a feedlot, and which are intended to be sold.

Field and row crops. Crops that are planted from seeds or transplanted from seed beds, and developed to the point of harvesting, typically within a few months.

Finance lease. A lease arrangement in which the lessee is assumed to have purchased the underlying asset.

Financial analysis. The examination of financial information to reach business decisions.

Financial accounting. A type of accounting that focuses on the proper recordation of transactions and the production of financial statements.

Financial instrument. A document that has monetary value or which establishes an obligation to pay.

Financial statements. A collection of reports about an organization's financial results, financial position, and cash flows.

Financing activities. The costs of loans and the income from investments.

Fixed assets. Assets that are expected to have utility over multiple reporting periods, and whose cost exceeds the minimum capitalization level of a business.

Forecasted transaction. A transaction that is expected to occur at a later date, but for which there is no firm commitment.

G

Generally Accepted Accounting Principles. A cluster of accounting standards and common industry usage that are applied to the recordation of transactions and preparation and presentation of financial statements.

Gilt. A young sow.

Grove. Fruit or nut trees that have been planted in configurations designed to facilitate their care and harvesting.

Growing crop. A bush, field, tree, or vine crop prior to being harvested.

H

Harvested crop. An agricultural product that has been gathered but not yet sold to a third party.

Hedge. An action taken to reduce an existing or expected risk.

Held-to-maturity security. A debt instrument that is acquired with the intent of holding it until it reaches its maturity date.

Horizontal analysis. The comparison of financial information across multiple periods.

I

Income statement. A financial statement that contains the results of an organization's operations for a specific period of time, showing revenues and expenses and the resulting profit or loss.

Intermediate-life plants. Plants that have a growth and production cycle exceeding one year, but less than those of trees and vines.

Inventory. An asset that will be consumed or sold within one year, as part of the normal operating activities of a business.

Investing activities. The purchase or sale of assets or investments.

Invoice. A document submitted to a customer, identifying a transaction for which the customer owes payment to the issuer.

J

Journal entry. A formal accounting entry used to identify a business transaction.

L

Land development costs. Consists of either permanent development costs, such as surveys, clearing, and leveling, or limited-life development costs that lose value over time, such as water distribution systems and fencing.

Lender. An entity that lends money in exchange for the payment of interest.

Livestock. Cattle, hogs, horses, poultry, sheep, and small animals bred and raised by an agricultural producer.

M

Managerial accounting. The collection, analysis, and reporting of information to assist management in making decisions.

Market livestock. Livestock being raised for sale.

Marketing cooperative. A cooperative that engages in the marketing of the crops produced by its patrons.

Member of an agricultural cooperative. An owner-patron of a cooperative who can vote at its corporate meetings.

Mid-month convention. The assumption that a fixed asset has been purchased in the middle of the month, and so will be depreciated for half of that month.

Multiple pool cooperative. A cooperative that calculates patronage refunds or net proceeds based on the results of separate commodities, departments, or accounting periods.

N

Net book value. The original cost of an asset, minus accumulated depreciation and impairment charges.

Net income. The excess of revenues over expenses.

Net realizable value. The estimated selling price of something in the ordinary course of business, with deductions for costs of completion, disposal, and transport.

Non-current assets. Assets that will be consumed in more than one year.

Non-current liabilities. Liabilities that will be settled in more than one year.

Nonexempt cooperative. A cooperative that cannot declare a tax deduction for a limited amount paid as dividends on capital stock and distributions to patrons of income derived from business with the U.S. government and non-patronage income.

Nonmember of an agricultural cooperative. A patron of a cooperative who does not have voting privileges.

Notional amount. The face value of a financial instrument, which is used to make calculations based on that amount.

O

Open pool. A pool that is not closed at the end of an accounting period. It is more likely to be used for crops that may require lengthy periods before they can be sold.

Operating activities. Those activities directly associated with running a business.

Operating expenses. All expenses incurred as part of the ongoing operations of a business.

Operating income. The excess of revenues over operating expenses.

Operating lease. A lease in which the lessee has obtained the use of an asset for a period of time.

Orchard. Fruit or nut trees that have been planted in configurations designed to facilitate their care and harvesting.

Order of liquidity. The presentation of assets in the balance sheet in the order of the amount of time it would usually take to convert them into cash.

Ordinary income. The income from continuing operations before income taxes, excluding discontinued operations and the cumulative effect of changes in accounting principles.

Other comprehensive income. Revenue, expense, gain, and loss items that are excluded from net income but included in comprehensive income.

Owner withdrawal. The removal of assets from a business by its owner.

P

Patron. Any person or other entity with which a cooperative does business on a cooperative basis.

Patronage. The amount of business done with a cooperative by a patron. This can be measured as the quantity or value of the commodities received by a marketing cooperative from patrons, or the quantity or value of the goods and services sold to patrons by a supply cooperative.

Patronage earnings. The excess amount of revenues over costs for those transactions that a cooperative engages in with its patrons.

Payables. The obligation to pay suppliers for goods and services that were acquired on credit.

Payroll. The compensation paid to hired employees, as well as the associated taxes.

Perennial crop. Crops that are alive all year, and which are harvested multiple times.

Permanent account. A balance sheet account whose balance is not cleared out at the end of the year.

Pool. An accounting concept used to calculate the earnings and patronage refunds payable to patrons.

Prepaid expense. An expense that has been paid for, but for which the underlying asset will not be entirely consumed until a future period.

Production animals. Animals that provide something that can be sold, other than their progeny. An example is sheep, which can be used to sell wool and meat.

Profit. The amount by which sales exceed expenses.

Progeny. The offspring of plants or animals.

Purchasing cooperative. A cooperative that buys, produces, and distributes goods and services to its patrons.

R

Retains. The amounts withheld by cooperatives from distribution to patrons. Instead, these amounts are allocated to the capital accounts of the patrons.

Revenue. An increase in assets or decrease in liabilities caused by the provision of goods or services to customers.

Revenue recognition. The process of determining the amount and timing of when revenue is recognized, based on the underlying earnings process.

Reversing entry. A journal entry that is the reverse of the original entry that was recorded in the preceding period.

S

Salvage value. The estimated amount for which a fixed asset can be sold at the end of its useful life.

Service cooperative. A cooperative that provides services to its patrons, such as accounting, data processing, storage, and trucking.

Single pool cooperative. A cooperative that calculates patronage refunds or net proceeds based on its overall operating results for all commodities marketed within an accounting period.

Sow. A female swine.

Glossary

Statement of cash flows. A financial statement that identifies the different types of cash payments made by a business to third parties (cash outflows), as well as payments made to a business by third parties (cash inflows).

Supply cooperative. A cooperative that supplies goods and services to its patrons that are then used in producing the products of the patrons.

T

Tax position. A position that an entity takes in a previously filed tax return or which it expects to take in a future tax return, which it uses to measure current or deferred income tax assets and liabilities.

Temporary account. An account in which transactions are accumulated for one year, after which the account is zeroed out and used again in the next year.

Temporary difference. The difference between the carrying amount of an asset or liability in the balance sheet and its tax base.

Trading security. A security that is acquired with the intent of selling it in the short-term for a profit.

Transaction. A business event that has a monetary impact on the financial statements.

Transfer point. The point at which an animal is shifted into a new category that has a different base value.

Trial balance. A report that lists the ending balance in each account.

U

Underlying. A variable, such as an interest rate, exchange rate, or commodity price, that is used to determine the settlement of a derivative instrument.

Unrealized gain or loss. The difference between the carrying amount and market price of a financial instrument that has not yet been sold.

Useful life. The time period over which an asset is expected to be productive.

V

Valuation equity. The difference between the cost and market value of certain non-current assets.

Vendor master file. The central repository of information about suppliers, which is used for payment processing and government reporting.

Vineyards. Grapevines that have been planted in configurations designed to facilitate their cultivation.

W

Working capital. Current assets minus current liabilities.

Written notice of allocation. A notification that states the dollar amount allocated to a patron by a cooperative, and the portion of that amount that will be issued as a patronage dividend.

Index

Made in the USA
Monee, IL
16 July 2024

61868339R00129